P9-DHQ-195

Elvis
A LIFE IN PICTURES

A LIFE IN PICTURES

TIM FREW

BARNES
& NOBLE
NEW YORK

ISBN-13: 978-0-7607-4619-6
ISBN-10: 0-7607-4619-2

Color Separations by Ocean Graphic International Company Ltd.
Printed in China by SNP Leefung

5 7 9 10 8 6 4

Dedication

To Susanne Frank, who is there for me in everything.

Acknowledgments

I'd like to thank Steve Slaybaugh, Sharyn Rosart, Chris Bain, and
Tanya Ross-Hughes for their help and support in the making of this book.

CONTENTS

Introduction

Above: In the early 1970s, Elvis began performing in his trademark flashy jumpsuits. Here he performs a song during the taping of the live television concert "Elvis: Aloha from Hawaii."

Opposite: Fans scream deliriously at the premiere of *Loving You* at the Strand Theatre in Memphis on July 9, 1957.

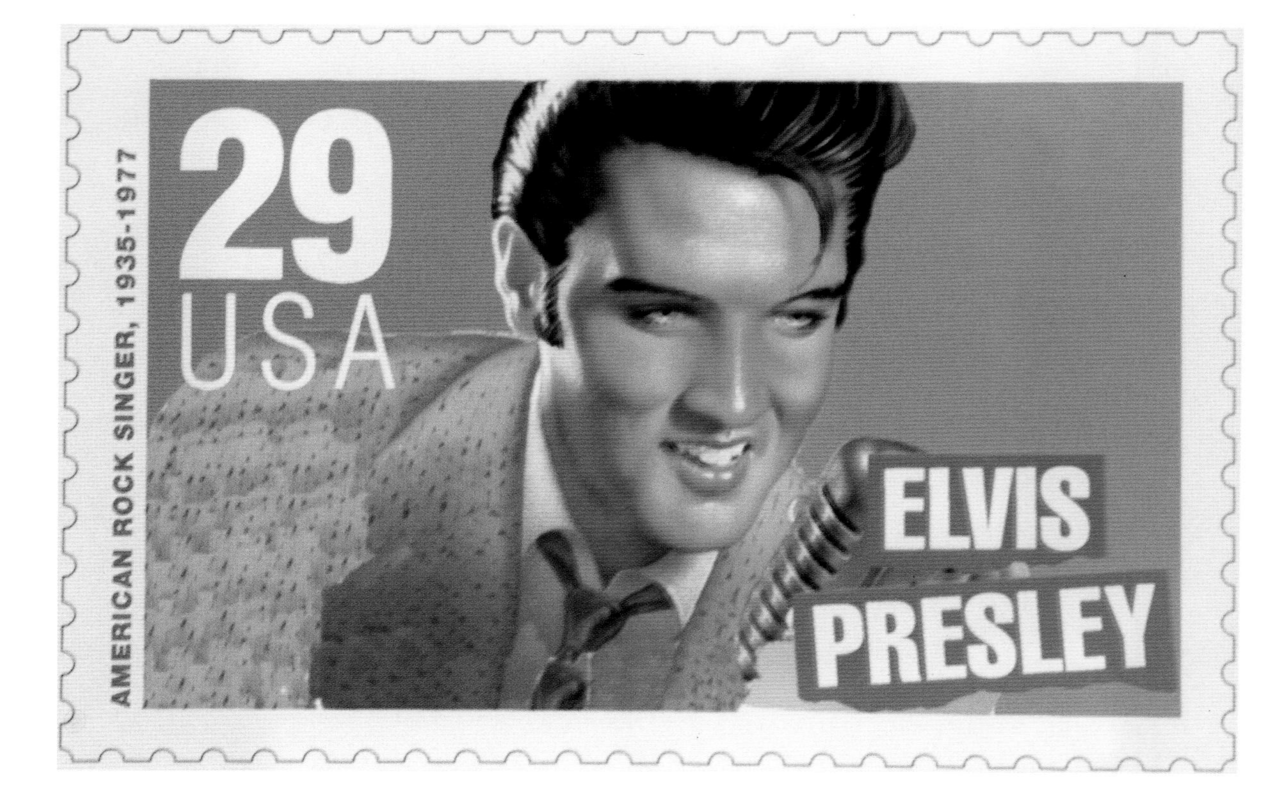

Elvismania has continued long after Presley's death. In 1993, the United States Postal Service honored the King of Rock and Roll with a commemorative stamp. After much debate about how Presley would be depicted on the stamp, the Postal Service let the public choose between an image of Elvis from the fifties and one of him from the seventies. The younger Elvis was ultimately chosen.

Elvis Presley is perhaps the most recognizable name of twentieth-century popular culture. Even two decades after his death, his records continue to sell; his movies still draw dedicated audiences; tens of thousands of fans visit Graceland every year; and his image and legend continue to figure prominently in books, movies, television shows, comedy routines, postage stamps, and, yes, even academic studies.

Elvis Presley is different things to different people. To many, he was the most exhilarating and revolutionary rock and roll singer ever to step onto a stage; to others, he was an overrated imitator of black rhythm and blues. To some he was (and is) nothing short of a spiritual icon; to still others he was nothing more than a self-indulgent entertainer.

When he first burst onto the scene in 1956, the *New York Herald Tribune* described Elvis as "unspeakably untalented and vulgar." *The Daily News* called him "appalling musically...suggestive and vulgar, tinged with the kind of animalism that should be confined to dives and bordellos." Religious figures and parents across the country viewed his music and stage antics as nothing short of obscene. The Reverend Charles Howard Graff of St. John's Episcopal Church in New York City described Presley as a "whirling dervish of sex." In a 1956 profile of the rock and roll phenom, *Life* magazine described Presley as "a different kind of idol...deeply disturbing to civic leaders, clergymen, and parents." Some radio stations flatly refused to play his records.

To the repressed teenagers of the 1950s, however, Elvis Presley was the epitome of teenage rebellion. He was six feet (183cm) tall and dangerously handsome. He wore his hair long and slicked back into a jet black DA. He radiated an open sexuality that was welcomed and admired by teenagers coming of age in a decade where conformity, obedience, and hard work were viewed as the only ways to get ahead, and where success meant a cookie-cutter house on a quarter-acre (1,012 sq m) plot in a planned suburban community. Presley was a poor Southern boy who snarled, wiggled, and sang his way to fame and fortune. In a time when many people's goals were to work hard, raise a family, and enjoy a life of secure anonymity, Elvis Presley stood up, curled his lip, thrust out his hips, and made the whole world take notice.

Yet behind the wild, thrill-seeking veneer, Presley was an honest, well-intentioned young man who drank nothing stronger than Pepsi, and addressed his elders as "sir" or "ma'am." He was a millionaire by the time he was twenty-one years old, yet he still lived with his parents in an unassuming, suburban house. In contrast to his arrogant and dangerous reputation, he always answered reporters' questions politely and was modest about his talent, even going so far as to say that he was aware that his voice was nothing significant and people came to see him play because of how he moved on stage.

With the help of a former carnival barker and self-proclaimed Kentucky colonel who went by the name of Tom Parker (his real name was Andreas Cornelius van Kuijk), Elvis Presley shot to

Much of Presley's early success was due to his electrifying live shows. Here, a young Elvis performs before a throng of adoring female fans at Russwood Park in Memphis, Tennessee. This concert took place on July 4, 1956, just two days after he recorded "Hound Dog" and "Don't Be Cruel" at RCA's New York City studio.

Elvis performs a song in *G.I. Blues*. The original title for this movie was *Café Europa*, after the Frankfurt nightclub where Lili (Juliet Prowse) was the featured performer.

superstardom in 1956. That year, he signed a lucrative contract with RCA; he had eleven singles in the Top Forty, including his first million-seller, "Heartbreak Hotel"; and his image was beamed into nearly every American living room with his appearances on *The Milton Berle Show*, *The Steve Allen Show*, and *The Ed Sullivan Show*. Presley also realized a childhood dream in 1956 by acting in his first Hollywood movie, *Love Me Tender*.

Originally titled *The Reno Brothers*, *Love Me Tender* was the first of thirty-one theatrical films Presley starred in between 1956 and 1969. The majority of these films were formulaic, some were highly entertaining, and many were downright dreadful, but all of them were profitable. From the time that he was discharged from the U.S. Army in 1960 until he made his infamous musical "comeback" in 1969, making movies, not music, was the central focus of Elvis Presley's career. During that period, Elvis recorded only four non-soundtrack albums—*His Hand in Mine* (1961), *Something for Everybody* (1961), *Pot Luck* (1962), and *How Great Thou Art* (1967)—two of which were gospel.

Parker took Elvis off the touring circuit because making movies was more profitable—Presley made three pictures per year at $1 million apiece plus fifty percent of the profits. While Presley remained famous throughout the sixties—the "Elvis Presley Picture" was practically a genre in itself—he was no longer an innovative force in the music industry. Gone was the rebel; Elvis was now mainstream. The songs he recorded for his movies were not much different than the Tin Pan Alley schlock that rock and roll originally rebelled against in the early 1950s. Rock and roll made great strides in the 1960s, but instead of being at the forefront of a musical revolution, Elvis was off in Hollywood essentially making the same movie three times a year for nine years. A studio executive purportedly once commented, "These are Elvis Presley pictures. They don't need titles. They could be numbered."

Parker told him once, "You stay talented and sexy, and I'll make us both rich as rajahs." Parker delivered on his promise—at the expense of Presley's musical integrity.

By 1968, Elvis saw his musical career slowly draining away. He had not had a number one single since "Good Luck Charm" in 1962, and while musical innovators such as Bob Dylan, The Beatles, and The Rolling Stones were breaking new musical ground, Presley was releasing such inane songs as "Queenie Wahini's Papaya" and "Yoga Is As Yoga Does." Elvis knew that if his career was to survive, something had to change. He decided to let the last of his movie contracts run out, and he went back into the studio to record quality rock and roll for the first time in nearly a decade. To mark his comeback, Elvis signed on to do a prime-time television special—his first public performance in eight years.

Thousands of fans line the streets of Memphis to watch the funeral procession of Elvis Presley.

"Elvis," which aired on December 3, 1968, was a triumphant turning point in Elvis' career. Trimmed down and clad in black leather, Elvis electrified his fans with the type of exciting, emotionally driven music that made him the "King of Rock and Roll" in the 1950s. In describing Presley's comeback, music critic Greil Marcus wrote, "If there ever was music that bleeds, this was it....He gave everything that he had—more than anyone knew he had."

More than a decade after he had made his debut, Elvis Presley began his second career as a rock and roll superstar. From the late 1960s through the early 1970s, the King was back on the top of his game. He was again recording quality songs, scoring Top Forty hits, and electrifying audiences with his stage show. Sequined jumpsuits, grandiose stage entrances and exits, a large supporting group of excellent musicians, and a chorus of background singers made an Elvis Presley show more of an event than a simple concert.

Throughout the 1970s, few artists worked as hard as Presley, who performed literally hundreds of shows a year across the United States. But the incessant touring began to take its toll on his health and state of mind. After his record-setting 1973 television special, "Elvis: Aloha from Hawaii," things swiftly went downhill for Presley. His decline into prescription-drug dependency grew unabated, and despite the constant companionship of female fans and his Memphis Mafia, Elvis became more isolated than ever. He stayed up all night every night, and slept everyday until 4:00 P.M. While on tour, he ordered the windows of his hotel rooms lined with aluminum foil to block out all sunlight. By 1977, he had given up trying to lose weight before going on tour, and his live shows were marred by his forgetting lyrics and his narcotic ramblings between songs.

Elvis Presley died at Graceland in Memphis, Tennessee, on August 16, 1977, leaving behind his ex-wife and child, Priscilla and Lisa Marie. Millions of fans around the world either mourned his death or flatly refused to believe that he was gone. In the history of American culture there has never been a figure as beloved, as revered, and as misunderstood as Elvis, and there will never again be anyone quite like him. Yet, despite his flamboyance, his idiosyncrasies, and his unbridled celebrity, at heart Elvis Presley was just a southern boy from Tupelo, Mississippi, who loved to sing.

> "I learned very early in life that, without a song, the day would never end; without a song, a man ain't got a friend; without a song, the road would never bend; so I'll just keep singing the song...."

—Elvis Presley, from his acceptance speech upon receiving his award from the Jaycees as one of the Ten Outstanding Young Men Of America, January 16, 1971

Chapter One

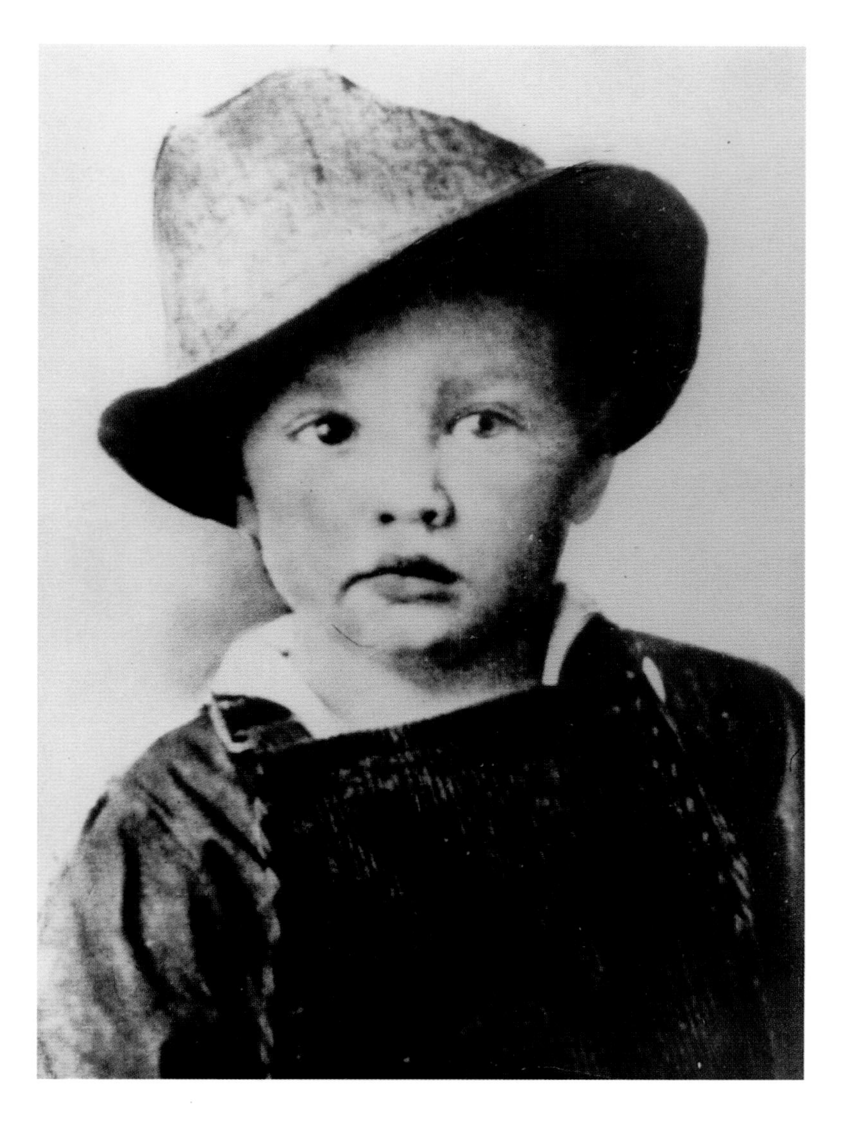

The Early Years

Above: Born into extreme poverty on January 8, 1935, Elvis Aron Presley (pictured here at the age of three) was the only son of Gladys and Vernon Presley of Tupelo, Mississippi. Elvis' twin brother, Jesse Garon, was stillborn.

Opposite: In 1957, Colonel Tom Parker commissioned Nudie's of Hollywood to design a gold lamé tuxedo for Elvis. While Parker loved the suit, Elvis hated it because it was too heavy, and he seldom wore both the jacket and pants. A photograph of Elvis wearing the entire tuxedo appeared on the cover of the 1959 album *50,000,000 Elvis Fans Can't Be Wrong—Elvis' Gold Records, Volume 2.*

On September 26, 1956, Elvis made a triumphant return to Tupelo, Mississippi, his birth place, where he performed two shows at the Mississippi-Alabama Fair and Dairy Show.

Right: Elvis poses with Bill Haley at Cleveland's Brooklyn High School auditorium on October 20, 1955. Haley's megahit "Rock Around the Clock," considered by some to be the first rock and roll song, hit number one on the charts on July 5, 1955. Presley's first number one hit was "Heartbreak Hotel," which hit the top spot in April 1956.

Left: In 1956, Elvis Presley signed a record-setting contract with RCA Victor, made several television appearances, toured incessantly, and quickly became the most famous rock and roll singer in the country. Here, proud parents Gladys and Vernon Presley go through one day's overflow of fan mail addressed to the King.

Above: Elvis used this custom-made, hand-crafted guitar for most of his early television appearances and live performances. This unique guitar was quite a change from the $7.75 model his mother had bought him for his eleventh birthday.

Opposite: In defense of his gyrating stage antics, Elvis said, "My manager told me that they [the audience] was hollering because I was wiggling. And so I went out for an encore, and I did a little more. And the more I did, the wilder they went."

Elvis gyrates in front of his band—Scotty Moore on guitar, D.J. Fontana on drums, and Bill Black on bass. Scotty Moore and Bill Black split with Elvis in September 1957 because of their low salaries; the two returned a few months later to record with Elvis until he went into the Army. D.J. Fontana remained Presley's primary drummer until 1969, when he left to become a session musician in Nashville.

Scotty Moore (left) picks and smiles as Elvis belts out a tune during a concert at the Stix Seattle Stadium in Seattle, Washington, on September 4, 1957.

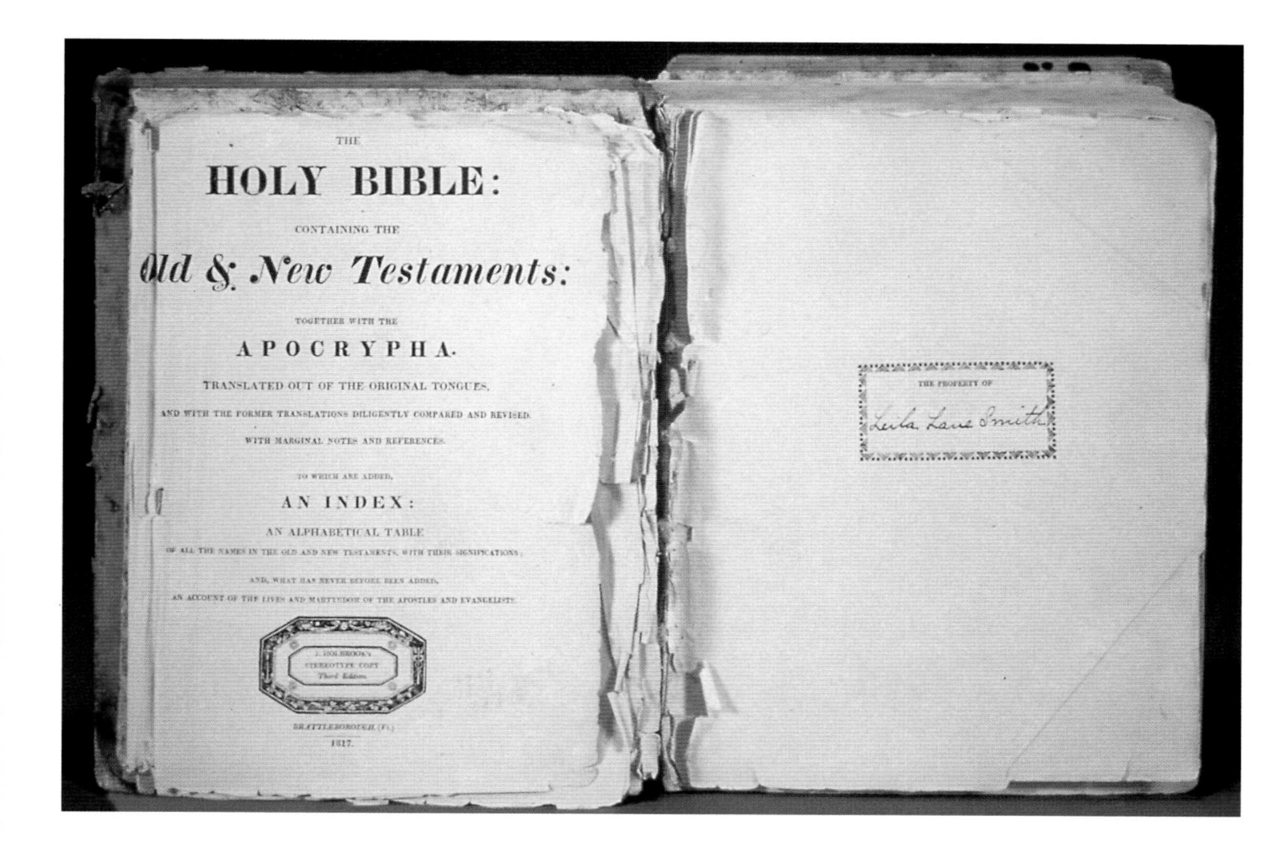

Left: A very religious man, Presley kept a Bible next to his bed at all times. This is the leather-bound Bible from Gladys' side of the family.

Below: Vernon and Gladys Presley pose in the living room of the first house Elvis bought, at 1034 Audubon Drive in Memphis. The Presleys lived there from May 11, 1956, to March 1957, when they moved to Graceland.

Opposite: Elvis rehearses with the Jordanaires (background) during a recording session at RCA's New York City studio.

Right: On November 20, 1955, Colonel Tom Parker (left) convinced RCA Victor A&R man Steve Sholes to pay $40,000 for the recording and publishing rights to Elvis. At the time, this was the most money ever paid for the rights to a singer.

Left: By January 10, 1956, RCA had Elvis in the studio for his first recording session. Presley would go on to sell more than half a billion records for RCA by the time of his death in 1977.

Below: The steady, driving beat of rock and roll music, combined with the dark and dangerous good looks of Elvis Presley, provided the perfect antidote for the sexual and social repression of the 1950s teenager. To parents, Presley was an out-of-control juvenile delinquent; to kids, he represented unabashed excitement and no-holds-barred rebellion. To himself, however, Elvis was simply a singer who was enjoying some unexpected success.

Left: Harking back to his days as carny barker, Colonel Parker blanketed towns in which Elvis was to appear with photographs, posters, pens, shirts, and many other types of promotional merchandise. In the early days, Elvis was very accessible to fans hoping for autographs. Eventually, however, his popularity was such that spontaneous public appearances became impossible.

Right: Elvis, whom Dewey Phillips once introduced as "the poor man's Liberace," met the sequined one himself on November 17, 1956, at the Riviera Hotel in Las Vegas. While Liberace played a toy guitar, Elvis held a candelabra and sang "Blue Suede Shoes."

Left: Elvis shows off the toy pistol he wielded during a dispute with eighteen-year-old marine Hershell Nixon in Memphis on March 22, 1957. Elvis claimed that he pulled the gun as a gag after Nixon accused him of bumping into Nixon's wife. Although Nixon initially swore out a warrant against Elvis, the two patched up the argument and charges were dropped.

Elvis with an unidentified guest and Ed Sullivan during a rehearsal for *The Ed Sullivan Show* on January 6, 1956. For this appearance Sullivan ordered that Elvis be shot from only the waist up in order to avoid the whole "pelvis problem."

Opposite: For his appearance on *The Steve Allen Show*, Elvis, at Allen's prompting, wore a formal tuxedo and sang "Hound Dog" to a floppy-eared basset hound. While accepting with good humor all of Allen's many attempts to humiliate him, Elvis later regretted appearing on that show.

Top, left: Of her relationship with Elvis, Natalie Wood said, "We value our friendship. We want to keep on being friends, but I dread the publicity we're getting because I know it can ruin a friendship. We're not in love. We are both eager about our careers, [and] too young."

Bottom, left: Elvis had to be hospitalized briefly during the filming of *Jailhouse Rock* in May 1957 when a dental cap came loose and lodged in the bronchial tube leading to his right lung. Here, Elvis shows nurse Beverly Altomare the front tooth from which the cap came off.

Above: In 1957, Elvis was introduced to Memphis deejay and television personality Anita Wood, and the two soon began a romantic relationship. Elvis and Anita (or "Little Beadie," as he called her) were nearly married on the eve of Elvis' departure for West Germany. However, Colonel Parker convinced Presley that he should remain single.

Below: By the end of 1957, it seemed as if nothing could stop the Elvis Presley juggernaut. He was already the country's biggest rock and roll star and, after completing three films, was fast on his way to becoming the biggest box office draw in Hollywood. But on December 10, 1957, Elvis received a letter from the Memphis Draft Board notifying him that he was up for the next military draft. Nine days later he received notice that he was to report for induction on January 20, 1958, the very same day he was scheduled to start filming his next movie, *King Creole*.

Opposite: Despite his relationship with Anita Wood, Elvis was accompanied by Las Vegas dancer and singer Dorothy Harmony when he reported for his preinduction physical at Kennedy Veterans Hospital in Memphis on January 4, 1958.

Chapter Two

Elvis in the Army

Above: Although he is shown here standing on a tank, Elvis was assigned duty as a jeep driver—the perfect duty for a man who loved cars as much as he did.

Opposite: According to those who served with him, Elvis never expected to be treated differently from the other soldiers and eagerly performed all the duties assigned to him.

After receiving a sixty-day deferment to finish the movie *King Creole*, Elvis reported to Local Draft Board 86 on March 24, 1958, to begin his service in the United States Army. The enlistment process turned into a media circus, carefully choreographed by Elvis' manager, Tom Parker.

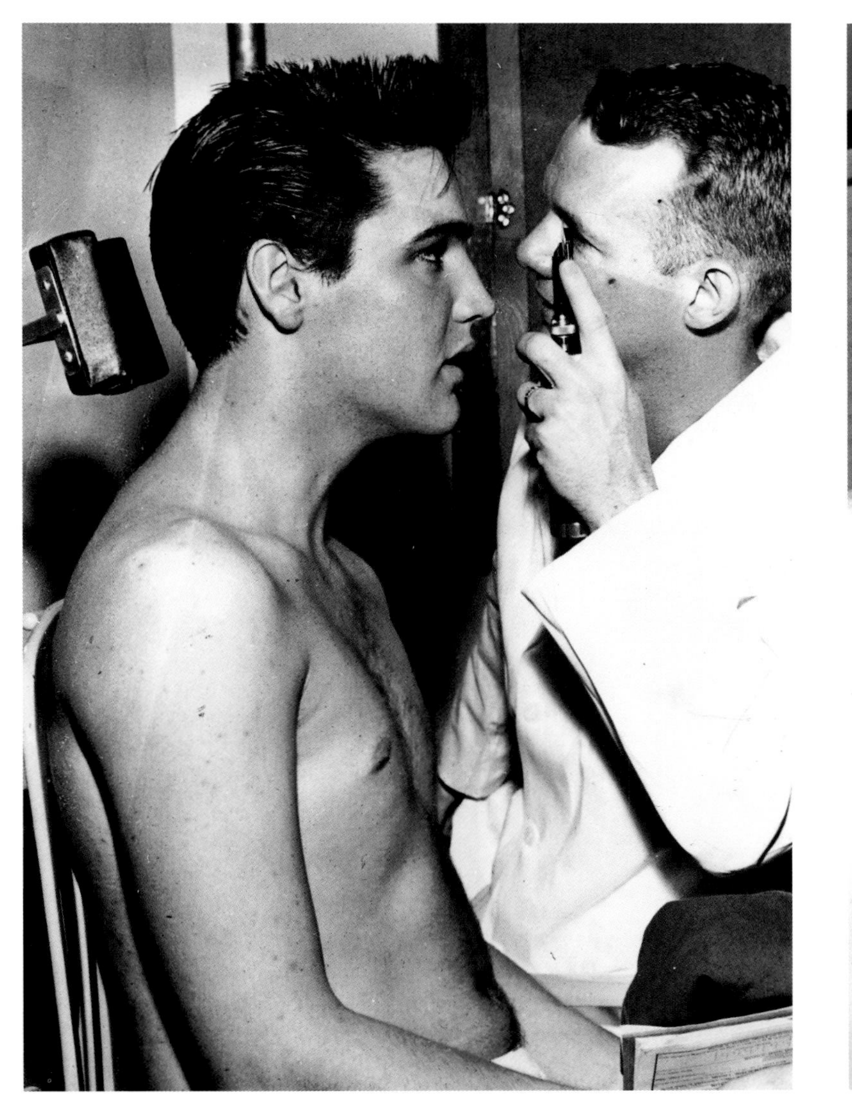

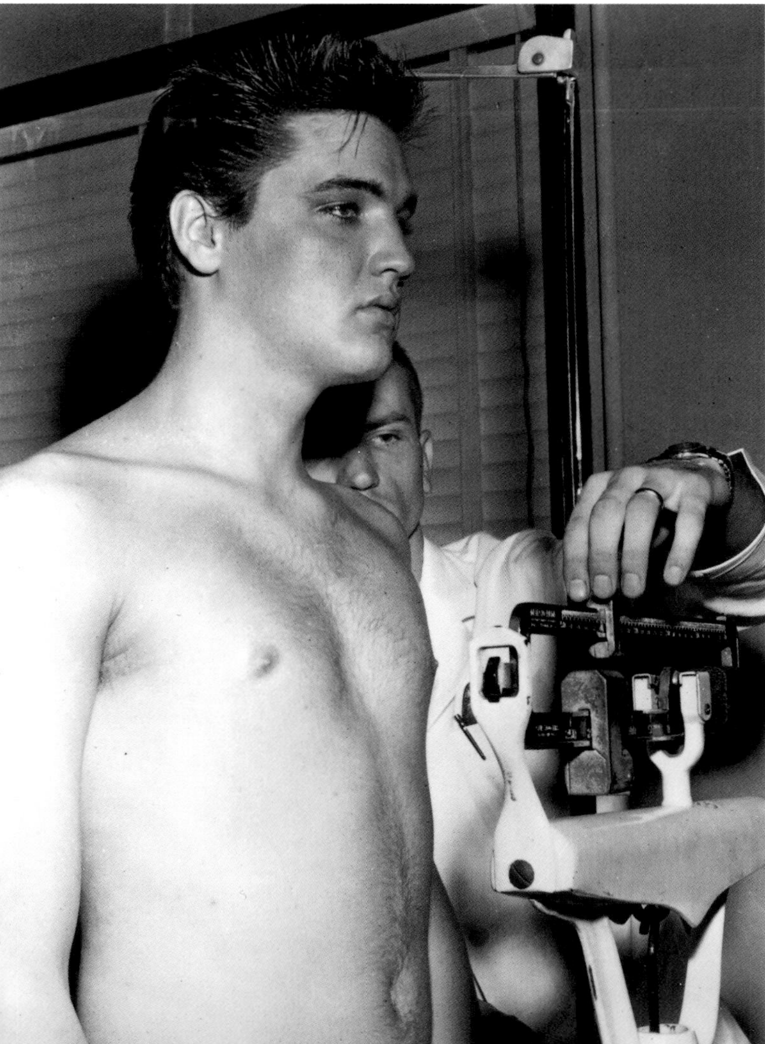

Above, left: Elvis is examined by a doctor during his army induction at Fort Chaffee, Arkansas. As a soldier Elvis earned $78 a month, much less than the $400,000 a month he was making as a rock and roll singer.

Right: Elvis smiles as he gets a shot during induction at Fort Chaffee, Arkansas. Despite his apparent calm, Elvis was worried that the public would forget him during his two-year stint in the army.

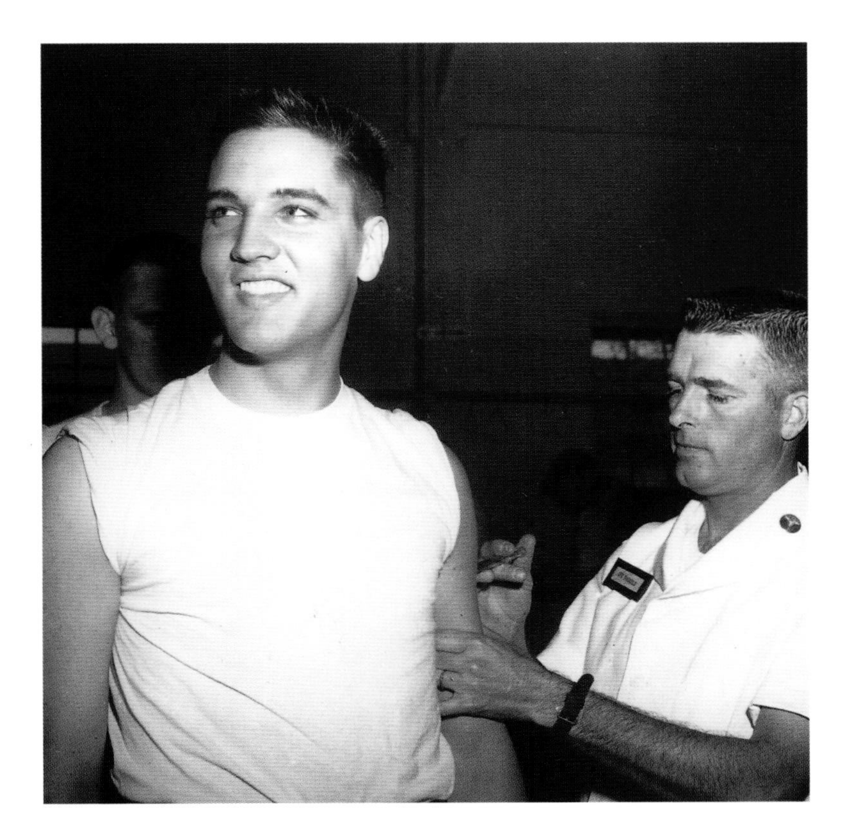

Above, right: Colonel Parker was able to use Elvis' army service as a public relations boon. Parker made sure that Presley would receive no special treatment, nor special assignments, to make his service easier. Elvis would go into the army just like any other recruit (except for all of the cameras and media attention) and willingly serve his country with great pride. Elvis weighed 185 pounds (84kg) when he went into the army and 170 pounds (77kg) when he was discharged two years later.

Above: When barber James B. Peterson of Guns, Oklahoma, cut Elvis' hair, the King of Rock and Roll quipped, "Hair today, gone tomorrow."

Left: Elvis Presley is officially sworn into the United States Army.

Opposite: Elvis collects his uniform and bedding as he is trailed by two other recruits and a stream of reporters and photographers. Presley spent just four days at Fort Chaffee, Arkansas, before he and twelve other recruits were bused to Fort Hood, Texas, for basic training.

Below: In September 1958, Elvis Presley and the fourteen hundred other members of his company boarded a train to New York for a brief layover before being shipped to West Germany aboard the USS *General Randall*.

Above: During Elvis' first leave from the army, he attended a preview of *King Creole* with his parents on June 6, 1958.

Above: Gladys Presley had to be hospitalized in August 1958 because of acute hepatitis brought on by a liver ailment. Elvis and Vernon discuss Gladys' ailment outside her hospital room on August 12, 1958. Gladys died two days later at the age of forty-six.

Newly promoted Private First Class Elvis Presley tries his hand at the accordion while en route to West Germany.

Right: Elvis poses in front of the Company D barracks in Friedberg, West Germany, on October 9, 1958.

Below: Elvis holds the hand of sixteen-year-old Margrit Buergin, whom he called "Little Puppy." Elvis met Margrit in a park in Bad Nauheim, Germany, and the two dated briefly, although she spoke only a few words of English. The press dubbed her the "German Junior Edition of Brigitte Bardot."

Above: A photograph of Elvis the soldier that Colonel Parker distributed as a Christmas card in 1958.

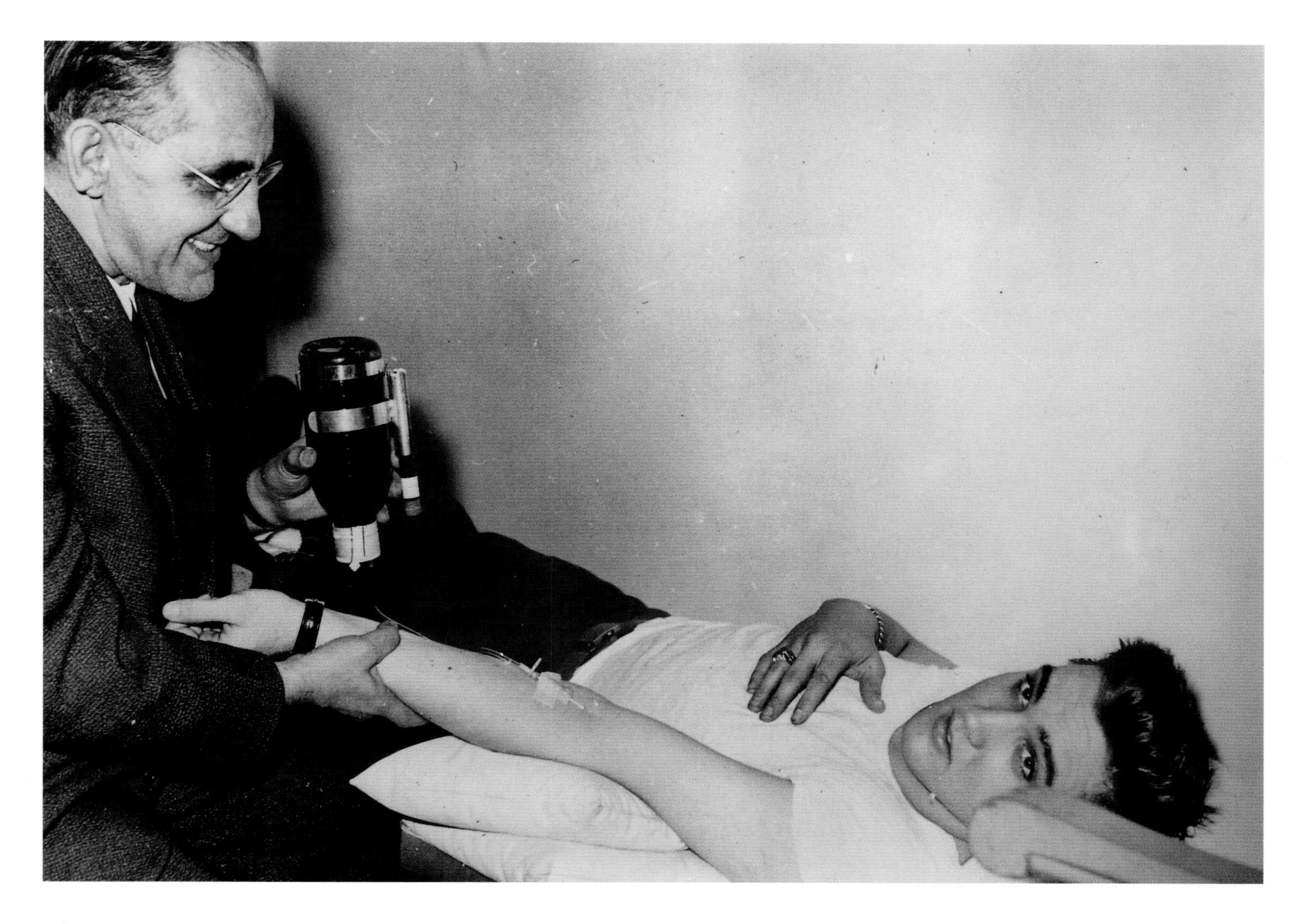

Above: An unidentified doctor holds a bottle of Elvis' blood on January 16, 1959. The singer was one of two hundred American soldiers who donated blood to the German Red Cross.

Left: Elvis achieved the rank of private first class on November 27, 1958, and was promoted to specialist fourth class on June 1, 1959. He was discharged on March 5, 1960, with the rank of buck sergeant, but in this picture holds an extra stripe up to his sleeve, giving himself the rank of staff sergeant.

Opposite: Elvis arrived at Maguire Air Force Base in New Jersey on March 3, 1960, during a raging snowstorm. Despite the predictions of the pessimistic press, the United States did not forget about Elvis while he was in the army. Thanks to the tireless promotional efforts of his manager and the judicious release of records Presley recorded before being drafted, Elvis was an even bigger star when he returned to the United States than before he left.

Right: Elvis fields questions from an eager press following his arrival from Germany. He stayed at Fort Dix, New Jersey, for forty-eight hours until he was officially discharged on March 5, 1960. Many of the questions pertained to "the girl he left behind" in Germany, fourteen-year-old Priscilla Beaulieu, daughter of Air Force officer Joseph Paul Beaulieu. Eight years later, Priscilla and Elvis would marry.

Left: Sergeant Elvis Presley lends an ear to actress Tina Louise, who was covering Elvis' army homecoming on the radio for the Mutual Broadcasting Network.

Elvis waves his discharge papers and muster-out pay after his release from the army.

Left: A happy Elvis Presley returns home to Memphis with Colonel Parker behind him. Parker never visited Elvis in Germany because the manager was an illegal alien in the United States, and was afraid that if he left the country he would not be able to return.

Above: A jubilant Elvis basks in the glory of his appearance with Sinatra, his first performance after his discharge from the army. Little did he know at the time that it would be his last television appearance and his second-to-last live performance for seven years.

Left: Just two weeks after arriving back in Memphis, Elvis headed for Miami Beach to appear in a television special with Frank Sinatra. Here, Elvis and Frank sing a duet, with Elvis singing "Witchcraft" and Frank singing "Love Me Tender."

Chapter Three

Elvis in the Movies

Above: Elvis as Johnny Tyronne in the 1965 movie *Harum Scarum*. The temple set used in this movie was originally built for Cecil B. DeMille's *King of Kings* (1926).

Opposite: Elvis takes a roll in the hay with Yvonne Craig (left) and Pam Austin (right) in *Kissin' Cousins*.

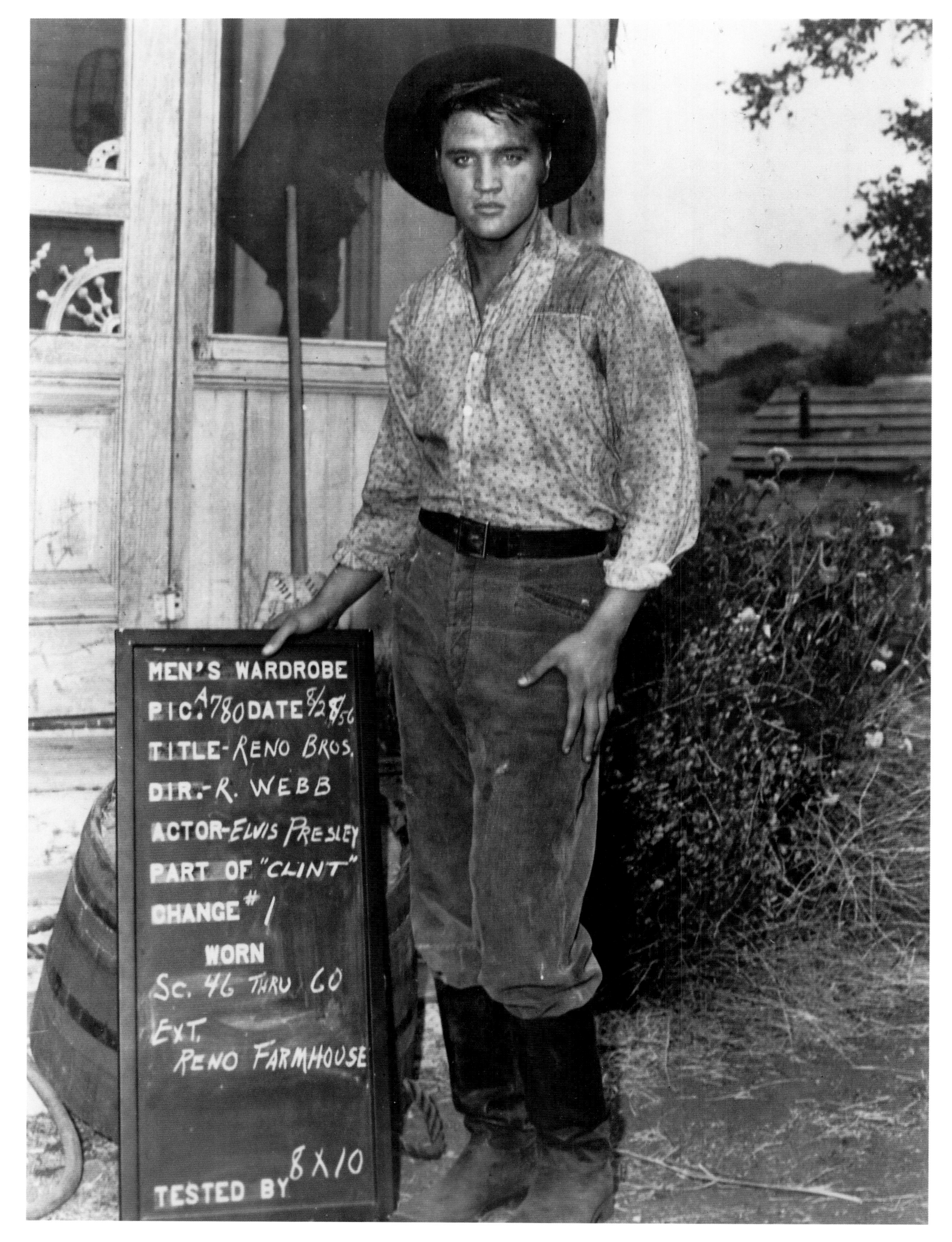
MEN'S WARDROBE
PIC. A780 DATE 8/28/56
TITLE-RENO BROS.
DIR.-R. WEBB
ACTOR-ELVIS PRESLEY
PART OF "CLINT"
CHANGE # 1
WORN
SC. 46 THRU 60
EXT.
RENO FARMHOUSE
8 X 10
TESTED BY

Opposite: Originally called *The Reno Brothers* (note the placard), the title of Elvis's first film was changed to *Love Me Tender* (1956) to capitalize on his latest hit single.

Above: Elvis and costar Debra Paget relax during a break in the filming of *Love Me Tender*, the first of thirty-three movies the rock and roll star made. Paget and Presley originally appeared together on Milton Berle's television show on June 5, 1956.

Left: Elvis draws his first paycheck as a movie star. His salary for the movie was a flat $100,000.

Right: Fans anxiously wait outside the Paramount Theater for the premiere of *Love Me Tender* on November 15, 1956. On the same bill was *The Girl I Left Behind*, starring Tab Hunter and Natalie Wood.

Below: *Love Me Tender* opened nationally on November 21, 1956. Despite the fact that Presley was the main draw in the movie, he did not receive top billing in the credits: Richard Egan and Debra Paget were both billed ahead of him. This was the only movie in which Elvis appeared that he did not receive top billing.

Above: Elvis talks to director Hal Kanter on the set of *Loving You* (1957).

Right: Elvis and Dolores Hart during a recording session for the film *Loving You*, Presley's second film and Hart's first. Hart made nine more films before retiring from acting in 1963 to become a nun.

Opposite: Elvis performing the famous dance sequence from *Jailhouse Rock* (1957). Much of this sequence was choreographed by Presley himself.

Right: Elvis takes a picture of Judy Tyler, his costar in *Jailhouse Rock*. Tyler did not live to see the film's release. She and her husband were killed in a car accident in Wyoming, on July 3, 1957.

Below: Judy Tyler gazes at a dejected Elvis in a scene from *Jailhouse Rock*.

Elvis in a crowd-pleasing shower scene from *G.I. Blues* (1960), the first movie he filmed after being discharged from the army.

Right: Elvis, as Danny Fisher, wields a knife in a publicity still for his fourth film, *King Creole* (1958). Directed by Michael Curtiz (*Casablanca*), *King Creole* was based on the Harold Robbins book *A Stone for Danny Fisher*.

Left: Angela Lansbury, Presley, and Roland Winters in a scene from *Blue Hawaii* (1961), the first of Elvis' Hawaii/ beach pictures. The movie was banned in Mexico because fans had torn up the seats and broken windows at the Mexico City premiere of Elvis' previous film *G.I. Blues*.

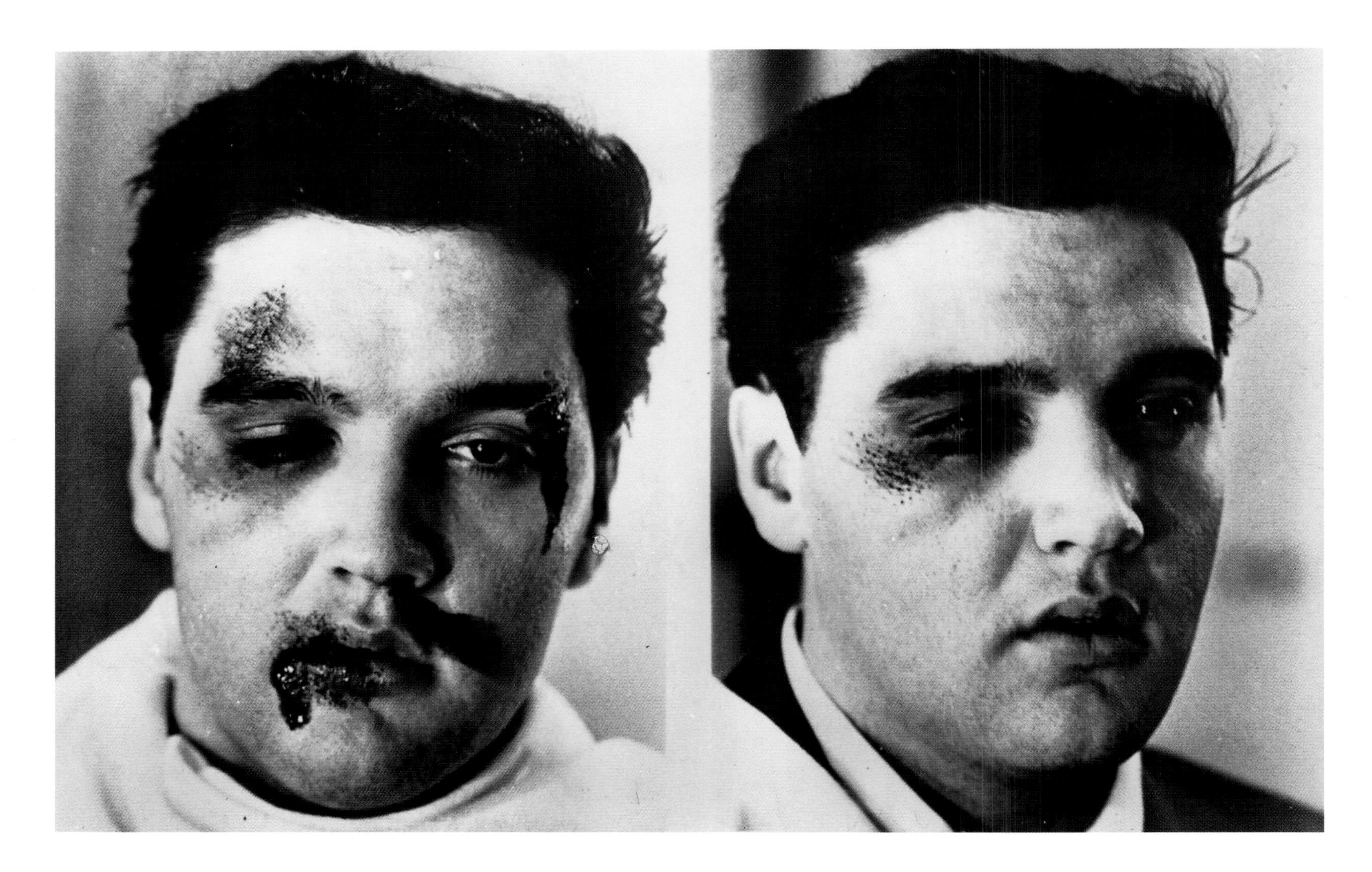

Above: The battered and bruised face of Elvis Presley is courtesy of United Artists' makeup department, not the result of a boxing-ring beating.

Opposite: For his role as boxer Walter Gulick in *Kid Galahad* (1962), Elvis took lessons from former junior welterweight boxing champion Mushy Callahan. Here, he squares off with Sugarboy Romero, played by Orlando de la Fuente, who in real life was an undefeated eighteen-year-old welterweight boxer.

Opposite: Elvis clowns around with Ginny and Elizabeth Tiu as actress Laurel Goodwin looks on in *Girls! Girls! Girls!* (1962), Elvis' eleventh film.

Left: Elvis and Joan O'Brien embrace in a scene from *It Happened at the World's Fair* (1963), much of which was filmed on location at the Seattle World's Fair in September 1962.

Below: Elvis meets The Four Amigos—Armando, Pedro, Pablo, and Sam—in *Fun in Acapulco* (1963). Although several location shots were filmed in Acapulco, Elvis never traveled to that city. All of his shooting was completed at the Paramount lot in Hollywood.

Below: In 1964, Elvis played both air force officer Josh Morgan (right) and blond-haired hillbilly Jodie Tatum in *Kissin' Cousins* (1964). To promote the film, MGM advertised that "Elvis has a blond-haired twin the gals swoon over."

Right: Elvis attempts to quiet a group of rowdy Texans in the Swingers Casino by singing "The Yellow Rose of Texas/The Eyes of Texas" in *Viva Las Vegas*, one of Presley's most popular films.

Elvis and Ann-Margret trade dance moves in *Viva Las Vegas* (1964). During the filming of the movie, the pair began a romance that Elvis ended after Ann-Margret announced to the press that the two were engaged to be married.

Above: Elvis negotiates a curve with Ann-Margret in a scene from *Viva Las Vegas*. When Ann-Margret would telephone Graceland she used the code name "Bunny." The code name was later changed to "Thumper" after the rabbit in the Walt Disney movie *Bambi*.

Left: In *Harum Scarum* Elvis plays a motion picture and singing star who is kidnapped while on a tour of the Middle East.

Below: Made in 1966, *Spinout* marked Elvis Presley's tenth year in films (it was his twenty-second picture). From left to right: Jack Mullaney, Elvis, Deborah Walley, and Jimmy Hawkins. Elvis briefly dated Walley, who had become the second movie "Gidget" when she made *Gidget Goes Hawaiian* in 1961.

Above: Elvis and costars Donna Douglas, Antony Eisley, and Nancy Kovack (left to right) in a scene from *Frankie and Johnny* (1966). The director, Fred de Cordova, had previously directed future president Ronald Reagan in *Bedtime for Bonzo* (1951).

Elvis, as Mike McCoy, performs with his band, 1 Plus 2 + ½, in the movie *Spinout*. In the movie he is pursued by four different girls, all of whom he marries.

Opposite: The filming of *Clambake* (1967) had to be delayed for several weeks because Elvis suffered a concussion when he fell in his bathroom and hit his head on the tub.

Right: Elvis sits atop a motorcycle in a scene from *Stay Away, Joe* (1968), his twenty-sixth film.

Below: In 1968, Elvis starred in *Speedway* with Bill Bixby (left) and Nancy Sinatra (right). Sinatra's character, Susan Jacks, was originally offered to British singing sensation Petula Clark, who turned it down.

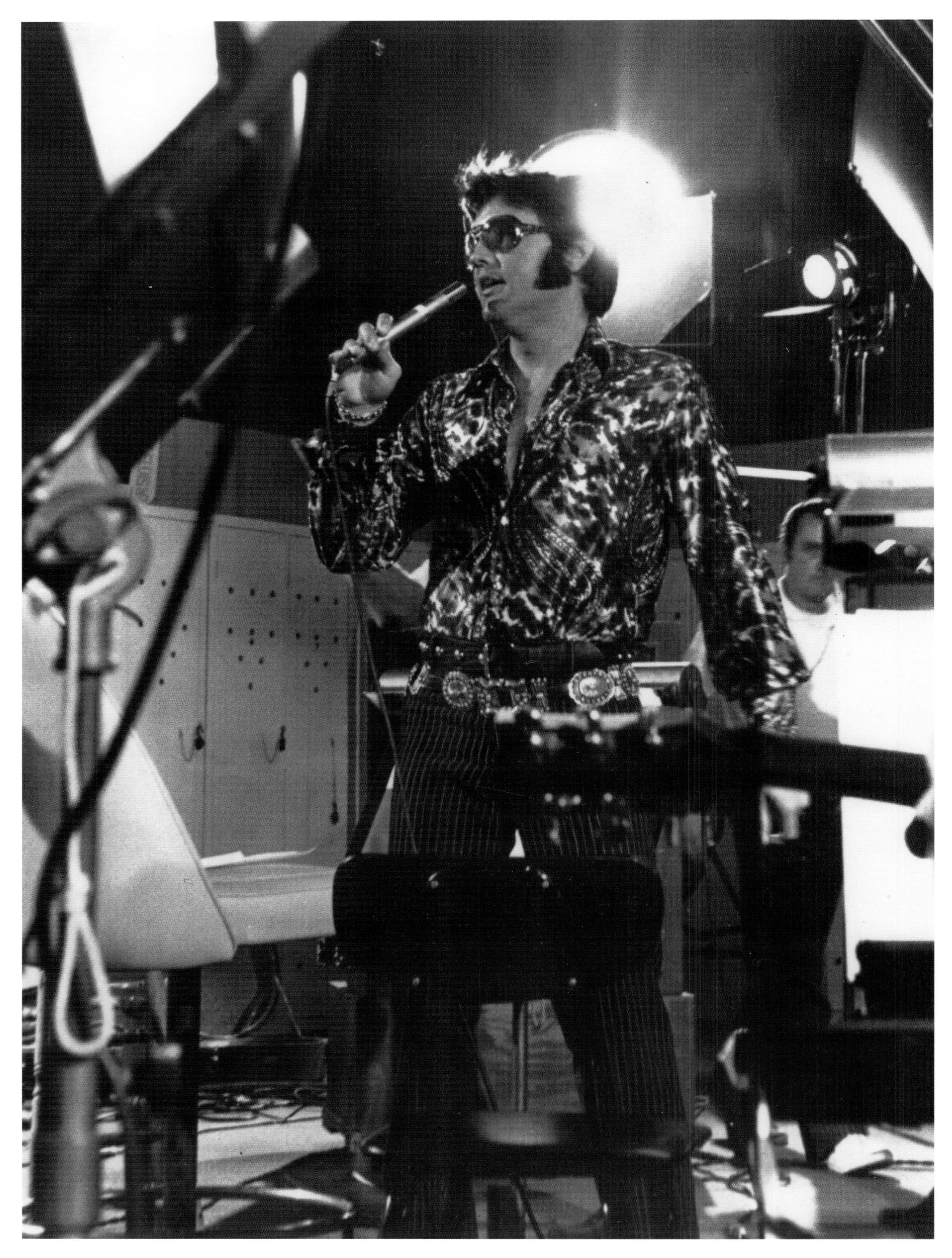

Above: *Speedway* was the third film in which Elvis played a race-car driver (*Viva Las Vegas* and *Spinout* were the first two)—a fitting role for a man who was a car fanatic.

Right: In 1970, Elvis was the subject of the documentary *Elvis—That's the Way It Is.* The film was centered around several shows Elvis performed at the International Hotel in Las Vegas.

Opposite: candid shot of the King from the 1970 documentary *Elvis—That's the Way It Is.*

Chapter Four

The Final Decade

Above: Presley's final resting place in Graceland's Meditation Gardens. Notice the spelling of Elvis' middle name. His birth certificate states his middle name as "Aron." Apparently, Vernon misspelled the name when he filled out the papers after his son was born. Elvis later had his middle name changed to the more conventional spelling of "Aaron." The discrepancy has been cited by those who theorize that Elvis faked his own death. They claim that Elvis had "Aaron" written on his tombstone because he was superstitious about having his real full name on his grave.

Opposite: As Elvis' dependence on prescription drugs increased, his battle with obesity became increasingly difficult. Here, he performs in 1977, just months before his death.

Below: Exactly nine months to the day after Priscilla and Elvis' wedding, on February 1, 1968, at 5:01 P.M., Priscilla gave birth to Lisa Marie Presley at the Baptist Memorial Hospital in Memphis.

Above: On May 1, 1967, Elvis Presley married Priscilla Beaulieu at the Aladdin Hotel in Las Vegas. Priscilla, who had been living at Graceland since October 1962, when she was seventeen, was one of the best kept secrets in Presley's life. Elvis' proposal was partially prompted by Colonel Parker, who was not sure how much longer he could keep Priscilla out of the press.

Right: In 1975, Elvis bought a blue-and-white Convair 880 jet and named it after his only child. The jet was equipped with a $14,000 queen-size bed (complete with seat belt), a conference room, four television sets, a bar, leather swivel chairs, and a pair of couches.

A bashful Lisa Marie hides her eyes as Elvis and Priscilla share a loving look.

Above: The present estate house on Graceland was built in 1839 by Dr. Thomas and Ruth Moore. Ruth was the niece of Grace Toof. Today, Graceland is a tourist mecca for Elvis fans around the world.

Below: In 1957, Elvis commissioned Doors, Inc., of Memphis to build the famous Music Gates at Graceland.

Above: Elvis poses at the front door of Graceland, his Memphis home for the last twenty years of his life. The 13⅓ acre (5.5ha) estate got its name when the original owner, publisher S.E. Toof, named it after his daughter Grace in the 1860s.

On December 3, 1968, NBC aired the television special "Elvis," later unofficially known as the "Comeback Special." This television event featured Elvis' first performance in front of a live audience in seven years. Here, he opens the show with a medley of "Trouble" and "Guitar Man."

Clad entirely in black leather, a trim Elvis catapulted himself back into the forefront of the music scene with an inspired yet very intimate performance. Colonel Parker had wanted the show to be a traditional Christmas special, but in a rare instance of rebellion against his manager, Elvis decided to follow his own vision.

Left: Elvis and Welsh singing sensation Tom Jones compare timepieces as Priscilla looks on.

Below: With his appetite for live performance whetted by the "Comeback Special" and his songs once again making their way to the top of the music charts, Elvis Presley signed on for two weeks of concerts at the International Hotel in Las Vegas beginning on July 31, 1969. The concert series smashed all existing Las Vegas attendance records.

Above: Elvis belts out a song at one of his shows at the International Hotel in August 1969.

Opposite: A trimmed-down Elvis performs during "Elvis: Aloha from Hawaii." This special was beamed around the world via satellite and at that time was the most-watched television event in history.

Above: On December 21, 1970, Elvis visited President Richard Nixon after showing up at the White House gate unannounced. Presley gave the President a commemorative World War II Colt .45 pistol and then convinced Nixon to give him a Narcotics Bureau badge. Who but Elvis Presley could arrive at the White House unannounced, carrying a pistol, and actually get in to see the President of the United States?

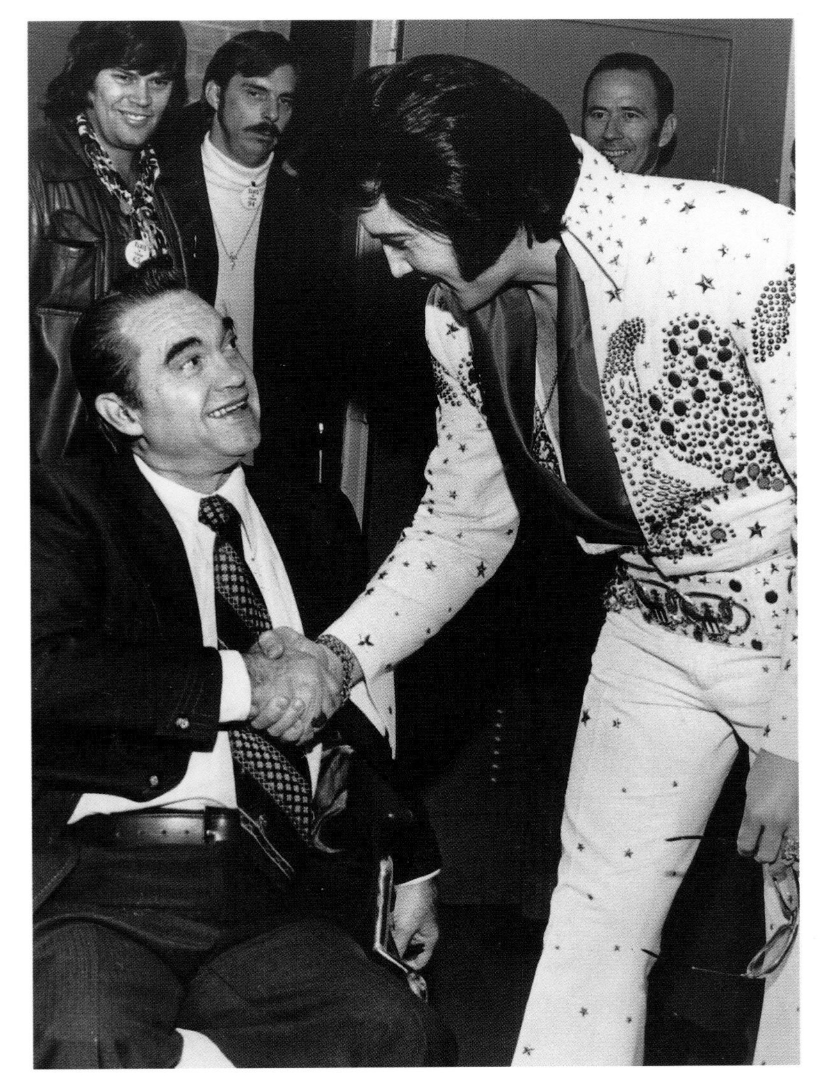

Right: Elvis shakes hands with Govenor George Wallace after a concert appearance at the Garrett Coliseum in Montgomery, Alabama.

Above: Elvis is joined on stage by a young Elvis Presley impersonator. Elvis continues to be loved by new generations of fans with each passing decade.

Left: TCB, which stood for "taking care of business," was Elvis Presley's business motto and working philosophy. The emblem was designed by Lee Ableseron, partner of jeweler Sol Schwartz. Elvis was buried with his diamond-studded TCB ring.

Opposite: A smiling Elvis makes his way through the crowd on his way to a concert appearance at Cincinnati's Riverfront Stadium in March 1976.

Pages 85–87: Throughout the 1970s, Elvis Presley maintained a grueling touring schedule, doing hundreds of shows a year. The incessant touring eventually began to take a toll on his health and his marriage. Elvis and Priscilla filed for divorce on January 8, 1973, Elvis' thirty-eighth birthday.

Above: Elvis Presley and Charlie Hodge arrive at Presley's house in Los Angeles.

Right: Since his days in the army, Elvis was a dedicated student of karate. He eventually held an eighth-degree black belt. Elvis encouraged Priscilla to take karate lessons—which worked against him when she attained a green belt and eventually fell in love with her instructor, Mike Stone.

ELVIS PRESLEY

DANGER
NO
SMOKING

Opposite: Immediately after leaving a concert appearance, Elvis is flanked by members of his infamous "Memphis Mafia."

Above: An exhausted Elvis signs an autograph in a snapshot taken by his bodyguard Dick Grob.

Above: Elvis Presley died at Graceland on August 16, 1977. The death was officially attributed to heart failure. Immediately after the news was announced, thousands of shocked and saddened fans converged outside the gates of Graceland to pay their respects.

Right: After Presley's death, his physician, Dr. George Nichopoulus, came under intense criticism for prescribing so many drugs to Elvis. Presley's last prescription included a dizzying array of pharmaceuticals: Dilaudid, Quaalude, Dexedrine, Percodan, Amytal, and Biphetamine.

Opposite: Pallbearers carry Elvis' body into a mausoleum at Forest Hills Cemetery in Memphis, where Elvis was buried next to his mother.

Conclusion

Opposite: Vernon Presley had the bodies of both Elvis and Gladys moved to Meditation Garden at Graceland on October 2, 1977, after an attempted bodysnatching at Forest Hills. Here, Vernon places a rose on his son's grave.

Left: This statue of Elvis, sculpted by Eric Parks and originally erected on Beale Street on August 7, 1980, was recently moved into the visitors' center at Graceland to protect it from the elements and vandalism.

In late August 1953, a teenage truck driver named Elvis Presley walked into the Memphis Recording Studios. This lucrative sideline to Sam Phillips' Sun Studios had the motto "We Record Anything—Anywhere—Anytime." Marion Keisker was running the studio that day. Elvis told her that he wanted to record two songs as a birthday present for his mother. Elvis would later admit that his mother's birthday was just an excuse—Gladys had turned forty-one four months earlier. "I went to Sun, paid my four bucks to the lady because I had a notion to find out what I really sounded like. I had been singing all my life and was kind of curious."

In an attempt to calm the anxious Presley, Marion Keisker struck up what is now a famous conversation with the future King.

"What kind of singer are you?"

"I sing all kinds."

"Who do you sound like?"

"I don't sound like nobody."

"Do you sing hillbilly?"

"Yeah, I sing hillbilly."

"Who do you sound like in hillbilly?"

"I don't sound like nobody."

The first song Elvis recorded was the early Ink Spots hit, "My Happiness." Midway through the song, Marion Keisker noticed something unique about Presley's voice and started a tape machine to make a copy of the young kid for Sam Phillips.

As Keisker told Elvis biographer Jerry Hopkins, "The reason I taped Elvis was this. Over and over I remember Sam saying, 'If I could find a white man who had the Negro sound and the Negro feel, I could make a billion dollars.' This is what I heard in Elvis...what they now call soul."

"My Happiness" was the first humble recording (Elvis described it as sounding like "somebody banging on a bucket") made by the poor, young Southern kid who would quickly become the most famous entertainer in the world. Elvis Presley would go on to

record hundreds of gold records, perform thousands of sold-out live shows, film thirty-three motion pictures, and inspire generations of future recording artists.

Born into the extreme, anonymous poverty of Tupelo, Mississippi, Elvis Presley lived the American dream to its utmost extreme. Yet, it was the very excess of his wealth and fame that led to his sequestered, eccentric lifestyle and his untimely demise. When the teenage Elvis walked into the Memphis Recording Studios, he may have been dreaming about becoming a singer. Maybe in his wildest dreams, he thought he could someday hear himself on the radio. The extent of his realistic expectations, however, were probably no more than just coming away with a nifty acetate he could show off to his friends. Even after he made his first "real" recordings and started touring the South with his band, Elvis' main goal was to make enough money to buy his mother a Cadillac.

Elvis Presley never set out to make millions of dollars, to spearhead a musical revolution, or to change people's lives. And he certainly didn't expect to become the cultural icon that he has. All he really wanted to do was to sing; the rest just seemed to follow naturally.

Discography

As the number of Elvis recordings continues to multiply, it would be difficult to compile a complete discography in the space of this book. Listed below are a selection of packages that will give readers a representative listening of Elvis' musical career.

Amazing Grace: His Greatest Sacred Songs. BMG/RCA: 1994.
The Complete Sun Sessions. BMG/RCA: 1976.
Elvis: His Life and Music. Friedman/Fairfax Publishers: 1994.
From Nashville to Memphis: The Essential 60s Masters. BMG/RCA: 1994.
King of Rock and Roll: The Complete 50s Masters. BMG/RCA: 1992.
NBC TV Special. BMG/RCA: 1991.
Walk a Mile in My Shoes: The Essential 70s Masters. BMG/RCA: 1995.

Filmography

Love Me Tender. Twentieth Century Fox: 1956.
Loving You. Paramount: 1957.
Jailhouse Rock. Metro-Goldwyn-Mayer: 1957.
King Creole. Paramount: 1958.
G.I. Blues. Paramount: 1960.
Flaming Star. Twentieth Century Fox: 1960.
Wild in the Country. Twentieth Century Fox: 1961.
Blue Hawaii. Paramount: 1961.
Follow That Dream. United Artists: 1962.
Kid Galahad. United Artists: 1962.
Girls! Girls! Girls! Paramount: 1962.
It Happened at the World's Fair. Metro-Goldwyn-Mayer: 1963.
Fun in Acapulco. Paramount: 1963.
Kissin' Cousins. Metro-Goldwyn-Mayer: 1964.
Viva Las Vegas. Metro-Goldwyn-Mayer: 1964.
Roustabout. Paramount: 1964.
Girl Happy. Metro-Goldwyn-Mayer: 1965.
Tickle Me. Allied Artists: 1965.
Harum Scarum. Metro-Goldwyn-Mayer: 1965.
Frankie and Johnny. United Artists: 1966.
Paradise Hawaiian Style. Paramount: 1966.
Spinout. Metro-Goldwyn-Mayer: 1966.
Easy Come, Easy Go. Paramount: 1967.
Double Trouble. Metro-Goldwyn-Mayer: 1967.
Clambake. United Artists: 1967.
Stay Away, Joe. Metro-Goldwyn-Mayer: 1968.
Speedway. Metro-Goldwyn-Mayer: 1968.
Live a Little, Love a Little. Metro-Goldwyn-Mayer: 1968.
Charro! National General Pictures: 1969.
The Trouble with Girls. Metro-Goldwyn-Mayer: 1969.
Change of Habit. Universal: 1969.
Elvis—That's the Way It Is. Metro-Goldwyn-Mayer: 1970.

Bibliography

Esposito, Joe, and Elena Oumano. *Good Rockin' Tonight: Twenty Years on the Road and on the Town with Elvis*. New York: Avon Books, 1996.

Frew, Tim. *Elvis: His Life and Music*. New York: Friedman/Fairfax Publishers, 1994.

Guralnick, Peter. *Last Train to Memphis: The Rise of Elvis Presley*. New York: Little, Brown, 1994.

Hopkins, Jerry. *Elvis: A Biography*. New York: Simon & Schuster, 1971.

Hopkins, Jerry. *Elvis: The Final Years*. New York: St. Martin's Press, 1980.

Marcus, Greil. *Mystery Train*. New York: Dutton, 1975.

Marcus, Greil. *Dead Elvis: A Chronicle of a Cultural Obsession*. New York: Doubleday, 1992

Marsh, Dave. *Elvis*. New York: Rolling Stone Press, 1982.

Presley, Priscilla, with Sandra Harmon. *Elvis and Me*. New York: The Putnam Berkley Group, 1985.

West, Red, Sonny West, and Dave Hebler, with Steve Dunleavy. *Elvis: What Happened?*. New York: Ballantine, 1977.

Photography Credits

Front jacket photograph: Photofest
Flap photograph: Howard Frank/Personality Photos, Inc.
Back jacket photograhy: Archive/©Frank Edwards/Fotos International (top); UPI/Corbis Bettman (middle and bottom)

Archive Photos: 2, 19, 23 bottom, 24, 30, 53 top, 59, 67; Fotos International: 79 middle, 84 bottom; ©Frank Edwards/Fotos International: 80, 86; ©Doug Preston: 86-87; ©Tony Rizzo: 71 bottom

Corbis-Bettman: 16, 20-21, 26-27, 44, 45 top, 93; Reuters: ©Rick Wilking: 10

FPG International: 35, 61 top, 92; ©Bernard: 28 top; ©Leon Dishman: 41; ©Dick Hanley: 52 bottom

Howard Frank/Personality Photos, Inc.: 6, 9, 14, 17 top, 18, 22, 25 both, 34, 36, 37 top right and bottom, 38 both, 39, 40 bottom right, 42 top and bottom right, 43 both, 47 all, 49, 50, 54, 55 top, 56, 57 both, 60, 62, 62-63, 64, 65 bottom, 66 both, 69 bottom, 71 top, 74 top left, 77, 78, 79 bottom, 81 top, 82 bottom

Retna: 75; ©Joel Axelrad: 85; ©Bonhams: 23 top; ©Holland: 48, 55 bottom; ©Dick Grob/Camera Press: 84 top, 89; ©Stephen Morley: 82 top; ©Doc Pele/Stills: 12, 61 bottom, 68, 69 top; ©Don Rutledge/Camera Press: 73, 76 top and bottom right; ©Tom Wargacki/Camera Press: 83, 88

UPI/Corbis-Bettman: 8, 11, 13, 15, 17 bottom, 27, 28 bottom, 29, 31 both, 32 both, 33, 37 top left, 40 top and bottom left, 42 bottom left, 45 bottom, 46, 51 both, 52 top, 53 bottom, 58, 65 top, 70, 72, 74 top and bottom right, 76 top left, 79 top, 81 bottom, 90 both, 91

Index

P9-CEV-524
BELIEVE.

ACHIEVE.

KILLER B's

ULTIMATE FAN EDITION

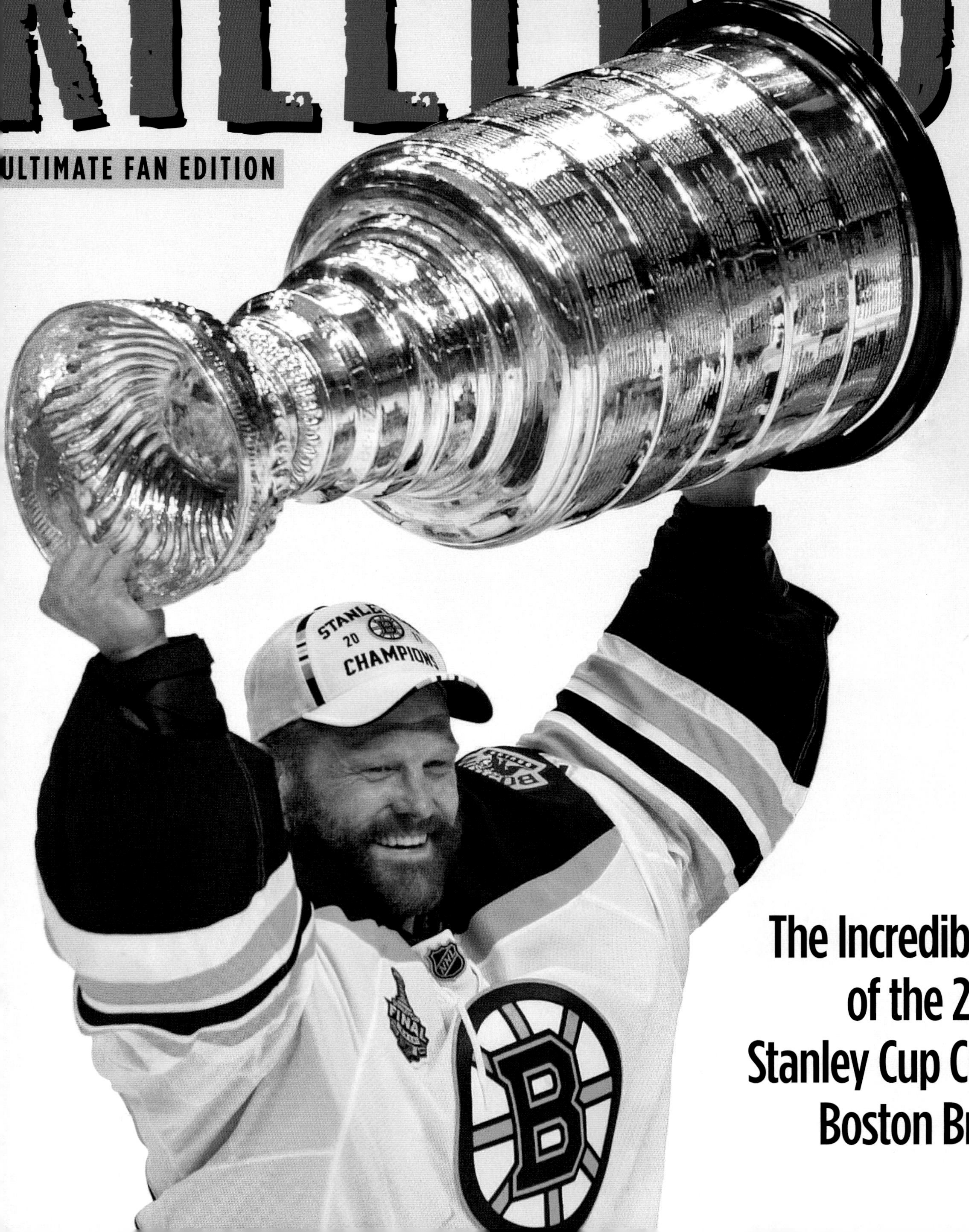

The Incredible Story
of the 2011
Stanley Cup Champion
Boston Bruins

CONGRATULATIONS TO THE BOSTON

COPLEY
COPLEY SQUARE
JCDecaux
Reebok
Ceaghlach

at&t
TICKETS & DEPARTURES
Museum of Science
Tours.com

MEMORABLE NUMBERS

798

Tim Thomas set records for the most saves in a single postseason (798) and in a Stanley Cup finals (238).

43

Mark Recchi retired at 43 with the fourth-most games played in NHL history (1,652) and is 12th all-time in points scored (1,533). He is also the only player on the Bruins roster who was alive in 1972, when Boston last won the Cup.

16

Bruins' captain Zdeno Chara led the playoff rankings with a plus/minus of 16.

11

Brad Marchand scored 11 goals in the playoffs to tie Jeremy Roenick (Chicago, 1990) for the second-most ever by a rookie.

2

The Canucks' Ryan Kesler, Henrik Sedin, and Daniel Sedin, who combined for 101 goals in the regular season, combined for two goals in the finals against the Bruins.

STANLEY CUP
20 11
CHAMPIONS
Reebok
BOSTON
19
FINAL
VAUGHN

The Boston Globe

This book is available in quantity at special discounts for your group or organization. For further information, contact:

Triumph Books
542 South Dearborn Street
Suite 750
Chicago, Illinois 60605
(312) 939-3330
Fax (312) 663-3557
www.triumphbooks.com

Printed in China
ISBN: 978-1-60078-701-0

BOOK STAFF

EDITOR Janice Page
DESIGN DIRECTOR Rena Anderson Sokolow
ART DIRECTOR Cindy Daniels
DESIGNER Jerome Layman Jr.
ASSISTANT EDITOR Ron Driscoll
WRITERS/RESEARCHERS
Mark Cofman, Rob Duca

PHOTOGRAPHERS

THE BOSTON GLOBE John Blanding, 167 • Yoon S. Byun, 15, 25, 33, 41, 108, 143, 156, 183, 189 • Charles Carey, 165 • Barry Chin, 7, 13, 42-43, 47-48, 54, 59, 67-69, 86-87, 94-95, 97-103, 139, 145, 152, 183-184 • Jim Davis, cover, 1, 16, 28, 34-39, 52, 55-58, 62, 74-77, 82, 119-121, 126-127, 129-131, 133, 138, 140-141, 143, 153, 192 • Jessey Dearing, 9, 24, 183 • Ted Dully, 162-163 • Bill Greene, 26 • Pat Greenhouse, 4, 183, 186 • Stan Grossfeld, 12, 18, 131 • Suzanne Kreiter, 154, 188 • Matthew J. Lee, 88, 141-142, 183 • Frank O'Brien, 160-161, 164, 167, 170-171 • Evan Richman, 167 • Dina Rudick, 60-61, 188 • David L. Ryan, 2, 182, 188 •John Tlumacki, 21-22, 38, 40, 42, 46, 50, 70, 72-73, 80-81, 88, 104-107, 113-117, 122-125, 128, 133, 137, 144, 151-154, 166, 172, 181, 183, 190.

ADDITIONAL PHOTOS COURTESY OF
AP/Wide World Photos, 11 (Bizuayehu Tesfaye), 12 (Brian Jones), 23 (Winslow Townson), 24 (Ryan Remiorz), 27 (Elise Amendola), 44 (Julie Jacobson), 133 & 184 (Charles Krupa), 138 (Katerina Sulova), 146 (Sean Kilpatrick), 148 (Kathy Kmonicek, John Ulan), 158-159 (file) • Aram Boghosian, 88 • Elsa/Getty Images, 60-61 (Harry How), 84 & 93-94 & 158 (Bruce Bennett), 133 (Eliot J. Schechter, Harry How), 148 (Dave Sandford) • Reuters, 34 (Mike Blake), 61 & 147 (Ben Nelms), 149 (Blair Gable), 150 (Shaun Best), 168 (Jim Bourg), 189 (Adam Hunger) • UPI, 109, 165.

With special thanks to Joe Sullivan and the Boston Globe sports department; Jim Wilson, Susan Vermazen, Stefanie Le, and the Boston Globe photo department; Jerry Melvin; Lisa Tuite and the Boston Globe library staff; Triumph Books.

CONTENTS

KEVIN PAUL DUPONT / Globe Staff

INTRO

The duck boats were queued up, their bows and sterns chock full o' Bruins. But before they pulled away from the Garden to start the rolling parade, team captain Zdeno Chara spontaneously decided to take the Stanley Cup to the crowd. Big Zee, hoisting hockey's prized trophy high over his head just as he had in wild-eyed jubilation only nights earlier in Vancouver, lugged it out onto Causeway Street much to the ecstasy of thousands of screaming fans.

The crowd roared. Boston's Stanley Cup moment, its first in 39 years, was officially underway on the bright and shiny Saturday morning of June 18.

An older woman, one who clearly lived through the '60s and '70s glory years of Orr and Esposito, Cheevers and Bucyk, surreptitiously broke from the crowd in tiptoed stealth. Holding a small camera with one hand, she inched closer to the obliging Chara and with the index finger of her opposite hand she ever so gently touched the Cup, her entire being seeming to melt upon making contact, and then like a giddy schoolgirl she neatly scurried back to the ranks of the hollering masses.

"I touched it,," said the overjoyed schoolgirl trapped in her AARP clothing. "I can't believe I touched the Stanley Cup!"

So hard to believe. So long to wait. And in the end, so much joy to be embraced and shared.

In the spring of 2011, Boston became a full-throated, chest-beating hockey town once more, its rubber soul (apologies to John, Paul, George, and Ringo) burnished and made whole again by a new cast of Black-and-Gold characters. Some four decades after they owned the city with the swashbuckling, heroic antics of the Orr era, the Bruins were back again to captivate and thrill, scratching and clawing their way past the likes of Montreal, Philadelphia, Tampa, and finally Vancouver to win the Cup for a sixth time in the franchise's storied, though oft-disappointing history.

"This is surreal," said a beaming Brad Marchand the night of June 15, in the moments immediately after the Game 7 championship clincher in Vancouver, where riots and flames quickly engulfed the streets of a defeated city. "It just doesn't kick in right now ... I don't know if it will ever kick in. We took everything they could give us. We took it and we took it, we played our butts off, we gave it back to them, and we won. We won the Stanley Cup." › PAGE 13

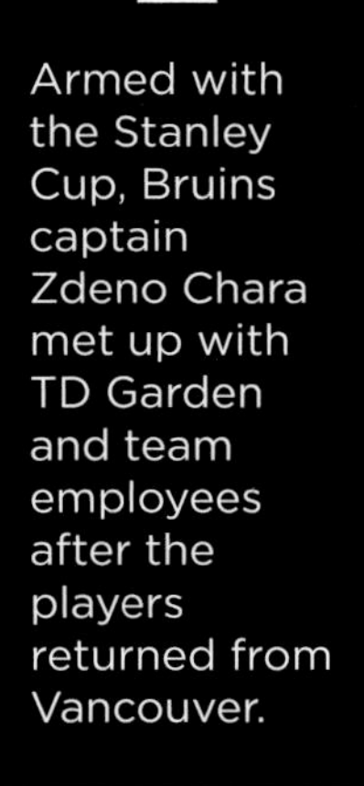

Armed with the Stanley Cup, Bruins captain Zdeno Chara met up with TD Garden and team employees after the players returned from Vancouver.

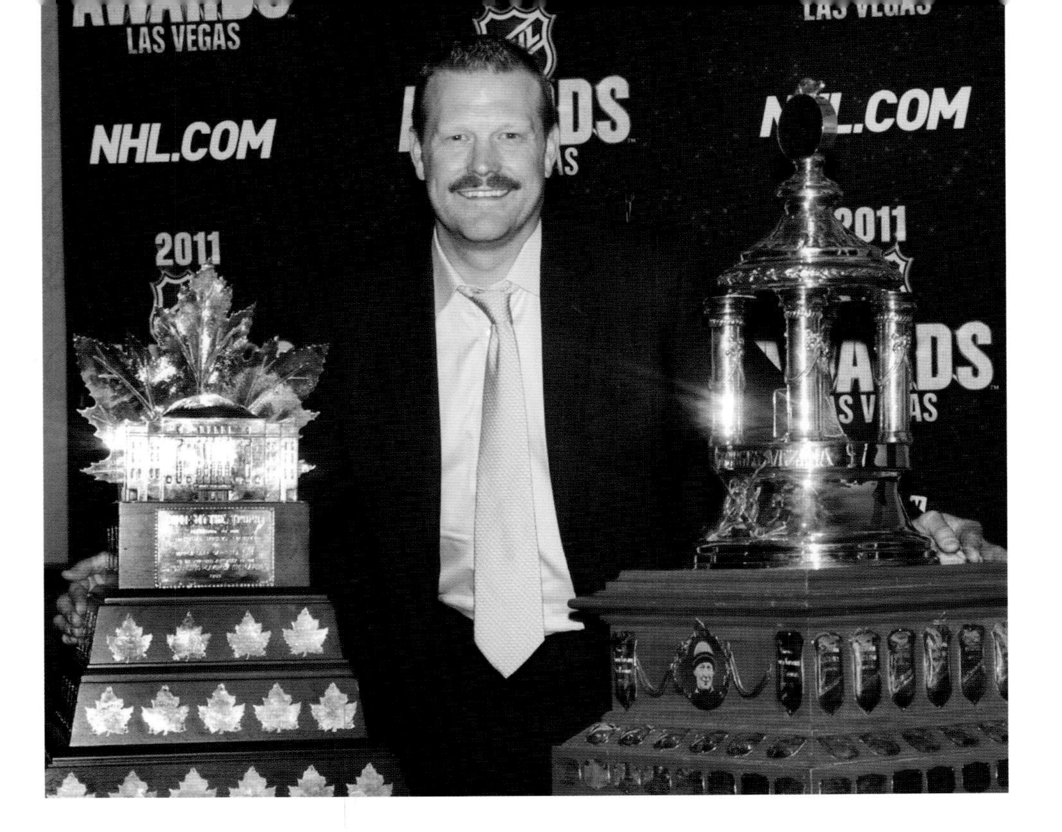

The play of Tim Thomas during the regular season and playoffs consistently was the difference in the Bruins' march to glory. At the NHL awards ceremony in Las Vegas on June 22, Thomas (right) posed with the Vezina and Conn Smythe trophies. Zdeno Chara (below) needed all of his 6'9" frame to give fans lined up and down Causeway Street a glimpse of the Stanley Cup during the Rolling Rally parade. Bruins center Patrice Bergeron (far right) had an opportunity to address the crowd during a pre-parade ceremony.

FROM 10 • The surrealism, the utter wonderment of it all brimmed out of Marchand. All championships carry a degree of wonderment with them, an initial moment of unbelievability, especially when the sport is so mentally demanding and physically grueling. The Bruins earned their crowns by grinding their way through the 82 games of the regular season, then 25 more in the playoffs, which included a league-record set of three Game 7 triumphs (Montreal, Tampa Bay, and Vancouver).

Across the 107 games, two of their top stars, Marc Savard and Nathan Horton, were rendered hors de combat because of concussions. Their power play, even with Tomas Kaberle imported as a would-be miracle maker, also never gained consciousness. And yet, they won.

"Resiliency," said general manager Peter Chiarelli. "More than anything, I think the players showed they were a resilient bunch."

Through it all, they became the ultimate survivalists, though undeniably gifted in their individual talents, none more so than playoff MVP Tim Thomas. The former University of Vermont sensation dominated the post-season in a way no goalie had since Ken Dryden led the Canadiens in the '70s and Bernie Parent led the Flyers earlier that same decade.

Only a week after winning the Cup and the Conn Smythe Trophy (playoff MVP), Thomas was awarded the Vezina Trophy as the league's top goaltender in the regular season, matching the award haul only won before by Parent when he was the stingy backstop of the Broad Street Bullies. Parent had his name etched on all three trophies in '74 and '75.

How different is today's NHL? For one, duck boats instead of Pontiac and Oldsmobile convertibles get rolled out for the Cup parade. For another, within minutes after Thomas won the Vezina, the 66-year-old Parent proclaimed on his Twitter account, "Congratulating Tim Thomas. Welcome to the club."

No, your daddy's NHL didn't Tweet.

"That's the stuff I enjoying hearing more than anything else," said a smiling Thomas, upon hearing of Parent's digitized valentine during the league's award ceremonies in Las Vegas. >NEXT PAGE

It took nearly a decade for Thomas to get his shot in the NHL after graduating from UVM. As a kid, he sold apples door to door in downtown Detroit to help put food on the family table. In his teen years, his parents hocked their wedding rings so he could attend a goalie camp and keep alive his dream of one day playing in the NHL. In the thick of the 2005-'06 season, with the Bruins desperate to patch their tattered net, they turned to Thomas only as a last resort. Now he's the first Boston goalie since Gerry Cheevers and Eddie Johnston to have his name on the Cup.

"It's hard to focus on all of it now because so much has happened," said Thomas while in Vegas for the award ceremonies. "I mean, I know it's all real, obviously ... and I think some of it not sinking in right away is because I'm tired, we're all tired. You know it's real because, hey, we did it, so you believe it. It just takes time to kind of absorb it all, I guess."

In one wild and wonderful eight-week ride, a franchise that opened its doors in 1924 (with out-of-towner Babe Ruth sometimes sitting in the Boston Arena stands) once again walked the champion's walk.

No falling victim to an arithmetical faux pas, such as when they were caught with too many men on the ice at the Montreal Forum in 1979.

No watching Petr Klima jump off the end of the Edmonton bench to stick a triple overtime dagger through their hearts in a hot and steamy old Garden.

No having nearly all the necessary parts, only to unravel due to their own spotty goaltending, or lack of a second scoring line, or wobbly-legged blueliners.

No watching Al Iafrate's knee give out, or Glen Wesley's shot ping off the crossbar, or one of Tim Taylor's skates slip a couple of illegal inches into Washington's crease. No glimpsing Bobby Orr's mortality on his way out the door to free agency.

Instead of NO!, the spring of 2011 was the season of YES! and WON! and DID IT! for the Bruins and their loyal fans. Too long accustomed to seasons ended in heartbreak, they lined up some million strong from the West End to Copley Square to share in a moment that was decades in gestation.

"I can't believe I touched the Stanley Cup!" said the woman with the camera and the little girl's twinkle in her eye. Perhaps not everyone could claim to have touched it, but everyone knew the feeling.

On the night of the final game, fans crowded around TVs at Boston's North Station when the nearby bars filled up.

JOHN POWERS / Globe Staff

CAN THEY DO IT AGAIN?

Perhaps it was a cosmic coincidence but when the Bruins won the Stanley Cup this year for the first time since 1972, they did it on the night of a full lunar eclipse, blotting out nearly four decades of shortfalls. The odds against them, in hockey terms, were astronomical. No NHL club ever had won three seventh games on its way to the championship and no Boston team ever had lost the first two games of a playoff and survived. This one did it twice. "You've been waiting for it for a long time, but you got it," goalie Tim Thomas proclaimed to the fans after he'd backstopped his spoked-B brethren to the most unlikely of their six titles.

Now, the question is whether the current Boston team can do what none before it has — hold on to Lord Stanley's mug. After the Bruins won their first championship in 1929 it took a decade for them to win another. When the 1941 club echoed that 1939 victory with a Cup of its own, who would have predicted that it would take 29 years for the next to arrive? Winning back-to-back crowns is devilishly difficult in the NHL. Since the New York Islanders won four in a row between 1980 and 1983, only Edmonton (in 1985 and 1988), Pittsburgh (1992), and Detroit (1998) have managed to retain their titles.

Expanded playoffs and longer travel have had much to do with that. These Bruins had to play 25 games and travel the equivalent of halfway around the planet to prevail. And salary-cap limitations have made it challenging to keep victorious teams together. After the Chicago Blackhawks won their first Cup since 1961 two seasons ago, they essentially held a yard sale, dealing away more expensive performers for cheaper ones. They ended up losing to the Canucks in the opening round of last season's playoffs.

The Boston front office, which had the foresight to lock up its key players, didn't have that problem going into the 2011-12 season with most of its biggest stars signed at least through next season. Losing key players is what doomed the 1972 club's chances of repeating after Gerry Cheevers, Derek Sanderson, Pie McKenzie, Teddy Green, and Ed Westfall departed either to the World Hockey Association or in the expansion draft.

That won't be an issue this season, when there's no rival league and no new clubs. These Bruins have an enviable stability with nearly all of the same players performing for the same coach in Claude Julien and following the same from-the-goal-out style with the same lunch-pail ethic and the same all-for-one culture that has distinguished this club since the Big Bad Bruins days of the late '60s.

Many of them are guys who'd once been overlooked or shelved or had bounced from club to club or been banged around in the minors, who hadn't won anything that anyone knew about and who wanted their name engraved on something prominent and permanent. They spent the summer showing off the Cup to thousands of people who'd never seen an ursine paw print upon it. But now the silver chalice is up for grabs again.

Everyone figured that the 1971 Bruins would keep the Cup in a bear hug until a most unlikely intruder snatched it away. Ken Dryden was a supersized rookie goaltender (and former Boston draftee) who'd played only six games for Montreal during the regular season and who spent most of his off-ice time studying law in the McGill library. But he snatched almost everything Boston shot his way in the opening series, prompting a frustrated Phil Esposito to call him a "(bleepin') octopus." When Dryden and his fellow Canadiens eventually hoisted the Cup, the Bruins already had been playing golf for a month. That's why it's hard for champions to repeat in the NHL. Sometimes a giant masked mollusk shows up with a glove.

WE ARE THE CHAMPIONS

4th
BOSTON
FIREWORKS
SPECTACULAR
www.JULY4TH.org
BOSTON 4 PRODUCTIONS
Courthouse
Parking
14921

BOB RYAN / Globe Staff

CELEBRATION TIME

Could anyone have concocted a more perfect fan scenario? En route to winning the Stanley Cup for the first time since Lou Grant was telling Mary Richards he hated her spunk, fans of the Boston Bruins watched their team ...

1 Break the hearts of their two most hated rivals — the Canadiens and Flyers — in completely different ways, the first by coming from an 0-2 deficit after losing the first two games at home, the second by dismissing the opponents in four a scant 12 months after they handed your team the most humiliating defeat in league history.

2 Outfight a gallant Tampa Bay team and its 40-something goaltender in a fasten-your-seat-belt series that culminated in one of the great hockey games any of us have ever been privileged to witness.

3 Spot the team with the league's best record two games and then win four of the next five by squeezing the life and very will out of them, finishing the job by shutting them out in their own rink.

All Stanley Cup wins are satisfying, but few have ever been won while traveling such a treacherous path. It was almost — almost — worth waiting 39 years to enjoy it.

So much for all the "alwayses" and "nevers." Did we all not tire of hearing how great the odds are against winning a series if you lose the first two games? Difficult is one thing. Impossible is quite another.

Yes, it's harder if you don't at least get a split of the first two. But it has been done; that's all anyone needed to know. Fans in Boston should know better than anyone, having lived through both sides of an 0-3 comeback in a six-year span. All these "alwayses" and "nevers" are true until they're not true. End of story.

Now we have a new one. No NHL team had ever won three Game 7s in one postseason. Well, now one has. Oh, and no team had ever shut out a team on the road in a Game 7. True Wednesday morning, absolutely. Not true Thursday.

History, Bostonians so love their history. Try this one. Consider the parallel between the NESN twins, the Red Sox and Bruins. Was there a lower feeling than the Aaron Boone home run, complete with the Pedro controversy? And what happened a year later? Euphoria! It was complete and utter revenge, accomplished in the most humiliating manner, correct?

OK, was there a lower feeling for Bruins fans than seeing the team blow both a 3-0 series lead and a 3-0 home-ice lead in Game 7 to the despicable team from Philadelphia? No way. A year later ... a sweep? Oh, there is a hockey god after all.

The 2004 Sox and 2011 Bruins win championships one year after suffering two of the toughest losses ever. We're barely worthy.

What a tremendous ride this was, 25 games spanning 63 days. So much happened, it's impossible to digest it all. Does anyone remember Zdeno Chara getting sick and missing a game? Didn't think so. Wait a minute ... didn't Patrice Bergeron suffer another concussion? Yes, yes, yes! Coming back to me now. And The Kid came in and got two goals, one of which reminded everyone why he was a No. 2 overall pick to begin with. Remember that?

Didn't they spend a couple of days in Lake Placid? Whose idea was that? Worked out pretty well, though, didn't it?

Mark Recchi went scoreless for 11 games and, c'mon, you know you said it; you, me, and half of New England moaned that he was too old and couldn't skate anymore, and how can Claude Julien keep him on the power play? And who was one of the best players on the ice in the final? Hint: We won't be seeing him anymore.

Claude, how about Claude? It was a universal assumption, rightly or wrongly, that he was going to get sacked if they lost to Montreal. Remember that?

You have to feel good for Claude Julien, a truly decent man who has his hockey principles and who now has the satisfaction of seeing his vision of how the game should be played result in the ultimate prize.

Winning the Cup is so hard, you know? Well, I guess we do know, since this team hadn't done it in 39 years. There were a lot of good players who couldn't get it done here – e.g. O'Reilly, Ratelle, Middleton, Park, Pederson, Milbury, Oates, Janney, and, of course, the hallowed Bourque.

And one of the very best of anyone's very best said that what he had just seen makes him appreciate what it takes to get your hands on that precious Cup more now than when he was wearing a Bruins sweater.

"I'm drained," said Cam Neely, once upon a time a stellar player and now a man with a key to the executive washroom. "I don't recall it being that way when I played. Now I realize what it takes to do this.

"It's so draining, physically for the players and mentally for us in suits. I'm mentally fried."

Think of how much more respect and admiration we have for some of these players now than we may have had before the playoffs.

Start with Brad Marchand. Hard to imagine anyone had him down for 11 post-season goals. He was a scrappy pup who matured into an alpha dog before our very eyes.

I mean, yeah, there were the hits and the Pie-like taunting of the Sedins and the other things that will make him a villain throughout the league. But did you check out that fancy-schmancy stickhandling as he went over and under and around and through Kevin Bieksa, a pretty good player, for his wraparound goal in the final? That's a hockey player, right there.

We could go on and on, but how about this one? Gregory Campbell. Make no mistake, Gregory Campbell's so-called "fourth line" turned around Game 7.

The Bruins were being outhit and generally outplayed in the first period when Campbell & Co. came on to play a dominating shift that monopolized the puck in the Vancouver end for about a day and a half and infused energy into the entire team. It was hardly a surprise when Marchand and Bergeron connected a short time later for the first goal.

Too bad they couldn't have given Campbell, sitting on the bench, an assist. We'll have to speak to Mr. Bettman.

That was no isolated incident. Campbell did things like that for the two months it took to win this Cup. He was the consummate "role player." As such, he symbolized what was so endearing about this team.

They really were a true T-E-A-M, seeking, and getting, vital contributions from the likes of Campbell, Shawn Thornton, Daniel Paille, Rich Peverley, and Chris Kelly, to augment the more publicized achievements of Chara, Dennis Seidenberg, Andrew Ference, Milan Lucic, Recchi, Michael Ryder, Nathan Horton, David Krejci, Bergeron, and Marchand.

As for Mr. Conn Smythe himself, perhaps the ultimate compliment came from one Mr. Glenn "Doc" Rivers, who was among the attendees at Game 6.

"Tim Thomas," said the Celtics coach, "is like having Bill Russell sit in front of the hoop without an illegal defense."

Sadly, far too much of what Bill Russell did to earn his reputation predated the videotape era. But every last second of what Tim Thomas has done continues to be there for us all to savor. The Sedin twins will forever be stonewalled, and Steve Downie probably thinks he's still going to score.

Ha!

BRIAN McGRORY / Globe Staff

DREAMING THE POSSIBLE

Welcome to the age of the possible in this happy little hamlet.

No, the Stanley Cup isn't going to get the unemployed guy a job. It's not going to pay anyone's rent when there's nothing left in the bank. It's not going to fix a broken marriage, or cure a sick child, or get customers through the door of a business that's slowly going broke.

But what it does, what this particular team has done better than any other in Boston since the lovable idiots of 2004, is to give the city and its people a super-sized dose of hope.

These Bruins offer the kind of narrative that the Red Sox, Patriots, and even the Celtics no longer have. They weren't supposed to win the title, like our other well-stocked teams generally are.

The bearded and burly 2010-2011 Bruins, more pitchfork than shrimp fork, did it the old-fashioned way — by outhustling, out-muscling, and outlasting every elite team that crossed their rough-hewn path.

In other words, they are exactly what our parents said would happen if we studied late enough, worked hard enough, and hung in long enough. Goalie Tim Thomas skated right out of a father's dream.

Hockey, too, is like that. It's not soccer, played on soft September Saturdays in suburban parks ringed by bright red and orange trees, convenient for one and all. It's not basketball in the warm environs of the high school gym on friendly Friday nights.

Hockey means getting up before dawn for rides to faraway rinks in the throes of frigid winters, or late nights trying to squeeze in ice time right before bed. Just getting to practice is a lesson in sacrifice — and often a family affair.

Which brings us to the Bruins and Boston. This is not exactly a golden age in Massachusetts, mostly because it's impossible to have any such thing in an economy this bad. But the Bruins are a blast from the past with a message about the future: Anything is possible. It's possible to rise above the dour national times. It's possible to break the bonds of middling expectations and grab what was assumed to be an unattainable prize.

Sports are, in many ways, about faith and identity. In Boston people invest enormous faith in the four major teams to do the right thing on the field and off. We wear their hats and shirts. We fill expensive seats to see them play. We learn the nuances of what our teams do better than any other set of fans in this land.

In return, the owners invest heavily, and the players provide reasons to identify with them through clutch performances, good deeds, and championships. We give them unparalleled support, they give us our swagger, and the city and its teams are all the better for it.

The day after the Bruins won the Cup, 79-year-old Lucia Flynn was sitting on the shaded stoop of a Mattapan apartment building waiting for a bus to take her shopping, still a little tired from the prior night's game.

"Pampered — that's the word!" she nearly shouted. "The Bruins aren't pampered! It feels great to see this happen to boys who worked so hard all year."

In that hard work and sheer will, they aren't all that different from the fans who watch them play. And that's why so many good Bostonians won't just reflect in the Bruins' glory, but see themselves in it as well.

All championships are great, but this one is special, the title that showed what's possible.

Bruins' fans were on top of the world, and also on top of a bus stop at Copley Square, when they turned out to cheer and trumpet all that passed by them in the victory parade.

A TALE OF TWO CITIES

The Bruins' Stanley Cup victory over the Vancouver Canucks isn't just a triumph for a team that too often lives in the shadow of other Boston sports franchises; it's also proof that Boston fans can celebrate with style. Well into the wee hours following the win, revelers crowded into bars and paraded around street corners with no major disturbances. If Vancouver didn't have enough to be depressed about, the senseless violence and looting that followed the Canucks' loss surely made their defeat more painful — and vindicated Boston's preparations.

"Killjoy" was one of the kinder accusations lodged at Mayor Menino after he decided that the TD Garden would not host a viewing party. Nor did he allow big-screen viewing in public spaces or other areas that would appeal to big crowds. In hindsight, Menino's decision seems sound.

Ensuring that there are limited opportunities for people to idly congregate is the first principle of crowd control. It is a lesson learned painfully by Boston police after Emerson College student Victoria Snelgrove was mortally wounded by a non-lethal bullet meant to disperse crowds after the Red Sox defeated the New York Yankees in the 2004 American League Championship Series.

With smaller crowds, public safety agencies had more resources to concentrate on the minor instances of aggressive partying in the region. Boston police also ramped up their visible presence on the night of Game 7. Their tactics — to keep the crowds moving, and to let celebrations occur but not for too long or on too large a scale — were evident throughout the area.

To be sure, several factors combined to make this celebration more manageable than some in the past. College students had graduated and left. The victory was in a faraway city. Victorious host cities often must confront vandalism and looting; Vancouver is the rare host city to lose a championship and then watch its fans get unhinged.

But there is much that Menino and his administration did to make sure that Boston's explosion was joyous and not riotous. The immediate announcement of a Saturday morning parade helped steer the focus to a weekend morning, in the summer, when the streets would be relatively clear of all but the revelers. And deciding to make it a rolling rally, as compared to a City Hall event, helps to spread out the crowd and let eager fans actually see the Stanley Cup.

It might have been nice to join friends and family at the Garden to watch the final game. But surely bringing home the Cup, with the city's reputation intact, is a lot nicer.

VANCOUVER

Following Game 7, some Canucks' fans rioted in the streets of downtown Vancouver.

In Boston, police formed a barricade to keep order near Haymarket Square.

IT'S A NEW DAY IN HOCKEYTOWN

Sirens wailed, air horns blasted, and the sky filled with confetti. Three days after the Bruins won the NHL's most coveted trophy, hundreds of thousands of raucous, roaring fans who had waited 39 years for this moment celebrated the return of the Stanley Cup to Boston with a giant, joyous Saturday rally for the city's latest champions.

The deafening throngs — a boulevard of Bruins' black and gold — packed in dozens deep along the parade route, filled nearby balconies, and watched from rooftops. They chanted "We got the cup!" as the victors rolled from the TD Garden, past Boston Common, to Copley Square.

Fans wore fake beards in honor of the Bruins' playoff facial hair, lofted their own Stanley Cups made of buckets and duct tape, and painted spoked B's on cheeks, chests, and fingernails.

The euphoric outpouring marked the return of the Bruins to hockey glory and the city's emergence as "Titletown" — the only city to win championships in all four major sports within a 10-year span. Once inevitably described as long-suffering or cursed, Boston was back.

"This is so exciting," said Mary McDade, a 49-year-old artist who snapped a photo with her cellphone as the coveted cup, held aloft by Bruins captain Zdeno Chara, passed her on Staniford Street. "I didn't know there were this many people in Boston, but we do love our Bruins."

Though victory parades are by now a familiar ritual in the city, this one seemed particularly charged with spontaneous moments.

Patrice Bergeron received at least three marriage proposals. Brad Marchand rapped along to Wiz Khalifa's "Black and Yellow." Chara marched with the Stanley Cup along the street, allowing a lucky few to run their fingers along the gleaming trophy. Before the parade even started, Chara arrived at the Garden on a bicycle, just a regular Joe at the top of his sport.

Tim Thomas, meanwhile, solidified his transformation from journeyman goalie to local legend, waving calmly to ecstatic crowds and brandishing the Conn Smythe Trophy he earned as the most valuable player in the playoffs.

"Thank you for your hard work," Matt Westling, a 27-year-old from Lexington, Massachusetts, shouted as Thomas rolled past him on a duck boat. "We appreciate it so much." Moments later, Westling hugged his friends, near tears. "Amazing," he said.

Police, who had estimated that 1 million people would attend the rally, did not provide a crowd estimate, and would not compare the multitudes to those who turned out for the Red Sox, Celtics, and Patriots' rallies. But many of the fans who attended those celebrations said this one felt like the biggest yet.

Some diehards had staked out spots on Friday afternoon, and the commuter rail had a record 120,000 inbound riders, nearly double the 67,000 who ride on a typical weekday. A number of commuters said they gave up because of delayed or crowded trains. Police made nine arrests, mostly for public drinking and disorderly conduct; the crowds were remarkably peaceful, if not exactly subdued.

Fans shouted "Loooooooch" — for Bruins forward Milan Lucic, who tipped his cap in appreciation. They chanted, "Let's go Bruins!" on packed Green Line trolleys. And they filled the air with the honking of vuvuzelas, the plastic horns that have migrated from international soccer stadiums.

Roaming through the crowds was a fan in a brown bear suit with a yellow polka-dot bowtie. Nine-year-old Tanner Holt of Seabrook, New Hampshire, wore an upside down Stanley Cup on his head, and a T-shirt that declared, "I've waited my whole life" for the cup.

Matt Brown, a 17-year-old Norwood High School student who has been in a wheelchair since January 2010, when he crashed headlong into the glass during a hockey game, was near the Garden, hoping to catch a glimpse of Bergeron. He said a Bergeron jersey, which the Bruins sent him after his injury, hangs above his bed. Watching the team's improbable march to victory, Brown explained, was an inspiration.

Also waiting outside the Garden was Normand Leveille, a former Bruin whose career ended when he suffered a brain aneurysm during a 1982 game in Vancouver. Leveille and his wife, Denise, drove six hours from Montreal to be at the parade.

The Bruins seemed as eager to salute the fans, as the faithful were to honor them. Several players delivered tributes at a pre-parade rally outside the Garden.

"You guys have been waiting 39 years for this," Bergeron said, brandishing the cup. "But it's here. And I hope it's here again, and again."

"We played together, we drank together, we lost together, and we never wavered," forward Mark Recchi said. "But the one thing we really did together: we won. One more thing: Thanks for the patience for the last 39 years. The next one will come a lot quicker."

One generous fan gave a Boston police officer a chance to hold his homemade Stanley Cup as the parade passed by Tremont Street.

BITS &...

BABY STANLEY

Bruins captain Zdeno Chara brought Lord Stanley's silver chalice home to his pricey condo at Boston's Union Wharf area, and the day after his team's victory he put the Cup in a baby carriage and took it for a stroll, posing for pictures along the way. Then he hopped onto his bike and headed to Firicano's Barbershop in the North End for a shave. "The beard was pretty thick," said owner Richie Firicano. "We used the electric clippers and then hit it with the straight razor. Took about 20 minutes to do."

MORE SHAVING STORIES

Milan Lucic and Johnny Boychuk also got the hot-towel treatment within hours of arriving home. Boston Barber Co. owner Robert Dello Russo said the players "almost went unconscious in the chair they were so tired." And then there was pragmatic Tim Thomas (below), who held off shedding his beard until he could do it as part of an event to benefit charity at Gillette World Shaving Headquarters in South Boston on June 20. "I don't know what I look like yet, but that's a lot of hair," Thomas said as he glanced at the carpet of clippings on his apron and at his feet. The Bruins' megastar goalie elected to spare his mustache, he said, "because my oldest daughter liked it."

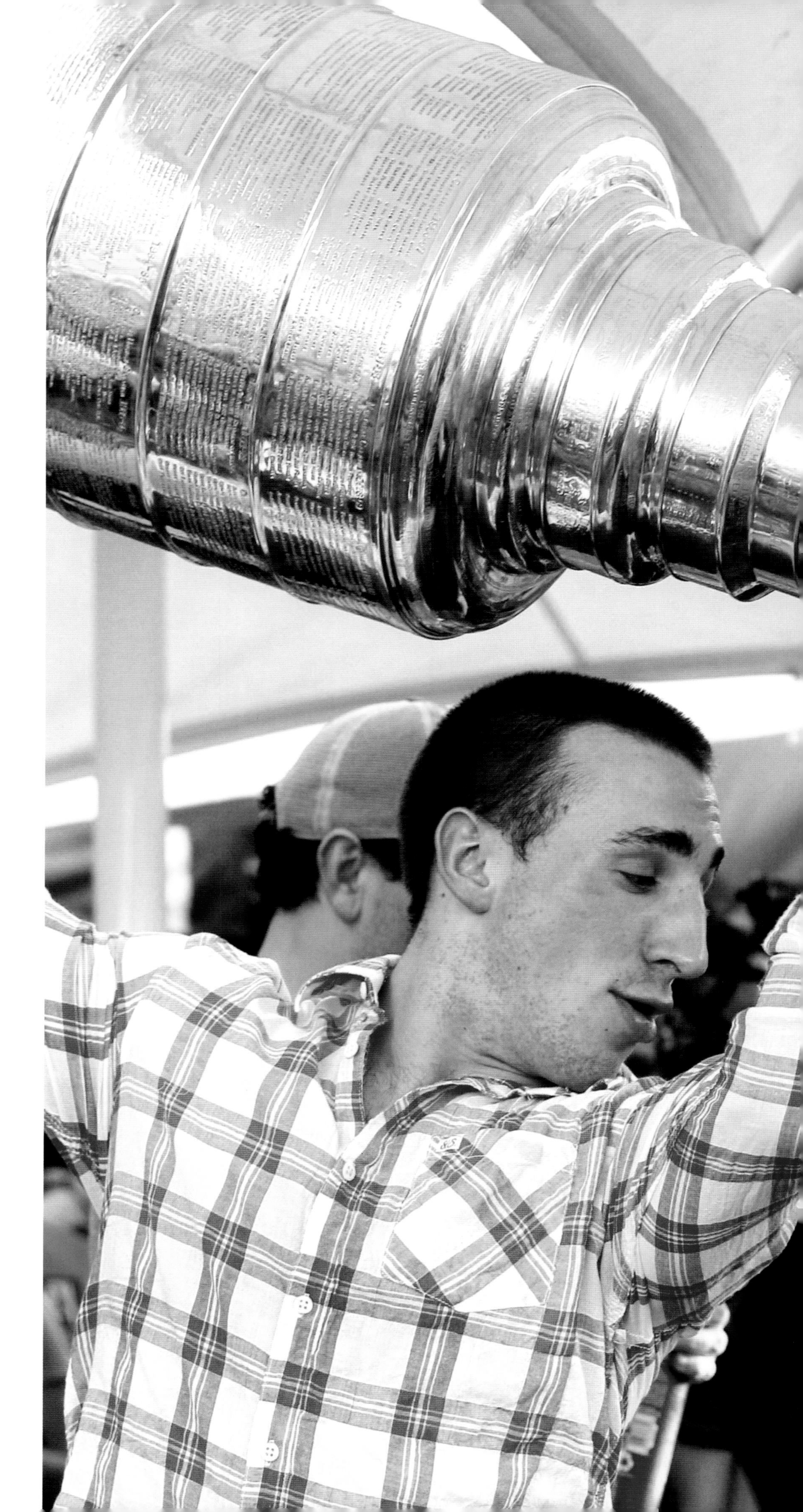

PIECES

$100,000 WORTH OF BUBBLY

In the days following their big win in Vancouver, members of the Bruins surprised diners all over the city by dropping in with the Cup at places like Tia's on the Waterfront (where Brad Marchand is pictured, at left) and Stella's in the South End. Two nights after winning their NHL prize, several Bruins brought Lord Stanley's king-size stein to Boston's Gypsy Bar, and the crowd went wild each time players lifted hockey's holy grail over their heads. (No, in case you're wondering, hearing Queen's "We Are the Champions" does not get old.) Following the next day's duck boat extravaganza, the B's boarded a bus and headed to Foxwoods for a no-holds-barred evening of bowling, bubbly, and boogying. They began the night at High Rollers, the upscale bowling alley owned by Big Night Entertainment's Ed and Joe Kane and Randy Greenstein, where the gleaming Cup sat on a leather couch next to Milan Lucic. From there, it was off to Shrine, where a section of the club was cordoned off for captain Zdeno Chara's crew. (Even the team's oldest player, 43-year-old Mark Recchi, jumped up on the bar and busted a move.) The highlight of all this hedonism, though, was a 30-liter bottle of Ace of Spades "Midas" champagne bought by the Kanes and Greenstein. Twice the size of the bottle bought by NBA owner Mark Cuban after the Mavericks won the NBA Finals, the crazy gold carafe cost more than $100,000. The full bill:

BAR TAB > $156,679

1 "MIDAS" CHAMPAGNE
A 30-liter bottle cost more than $100,000

136
Bud Lights

35
Jager Bombs

9
bottles Goose MG

3
bottles Captain Morgan

1
Amstel Light

AL EAST
W L GB
BOSTON 42 28 —
NEW YORK 40 29 1 ½
TAMPA BAY 38 33 4 ½
TORONTO 36 35 6 ½
BALTIMORE 31 37 10
minute clinic
CVS/pharmacy
310
Budweiser Budweiser

Fresh from their Cup win four days earlier, a line of Bruins tossed out ceremonial first pitches at Fenway, where the Red Sox were hosting the Milwaukee Brewers.

VERSUS VANCOUVER

DESTINY

The Bruins decided that the script for this Stanley Cup drama was getting a bit formulaic: close, gnawing defeats in the Pacific Northwest followed by dominating victories at home. So they rewrote the ending and joined the Cup legacies of Shore, Schmidt, and Orr.

CANUCKS BRUINS

Game 1

1-0

BOS	0	0	0	0
VAN	0	0	1	1

WEDNESDAY, JUNE 1, 2011 • **VANCOUVER**

Game 2

3-2

BOS	0	2	0	0	2
VAN	1	0	1	1	3

SATURDAY, JUNE 4, 2011 • **VANCOUVER**

Game 3

8-1

VAN	0	0	1	1
BOS	0	4	4	8

MONDAY, JUNE 6, 2011 • **BOSTON**

Game 4

4-0

VAN	0	0	0	0
BOS	1	2	1	4

WEDNESDAY, JUNE 8, 2011 • **BOSTON**

Game 5

1-0

BOS	0	0	0	0
VAN	0	0	1	1

FRIDAY, JUNE 10, 2011 • **VANCOUVER**

Game 6

5-2

VAN	0	0	2	2
BOS	4	0	1	5

MONDAY, JUNE 13, 2011 • **BOSTON**

Game 7

4-0

BOS	1	2	1	4
VAN	0	0	0	0

WEDNESDAY, JUNE 15, 2011 • **VANCOUVER**

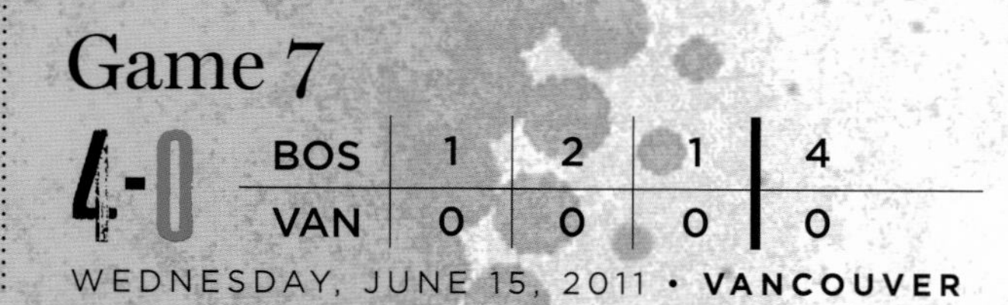

FINAL

THE CUP

They won it for every New England mom and dad who ever woke up to drive kids to the rink at 6 a.m., and drank hot chocolate while they waited in the cold. They won it for the Revere girls with the big hair and O'Reilly sweaters; for the shot-and-beer guys who pour every dollar of expendable income into the hockey budget. They won it to avenge losing Bobby Orr to Chicago, too many men on the ice in Montreal, free agents never signed, trades that went bad, unspeakable injuries, and Game 7 disappointments. They won it for you.

The Boston Bruins won the Stanley Cup, shocking the Vancouver Canucks, 4-0, capping an epic seven-game series and bringing the holy grail to the Hub of Hockey for the first time since 1972. The goals were scored by Patrice Bergeron and Brad (Little Ball Of Hate) Marchand, two apiece. The non-goals were stopped by playoff MVP Tim Thomas.

Everyman Thomas is now Tom Brady, Bill Russell, and Curt Schilling. And the Bruins are Stanley Cup champs. They outscored the favored Canucks by a whopping 23-8 over seven games. Thomas addressed Cup-starved Boston fans, saying, "You've been waiting for it a long time, but you got it. You wanted it, you got it. We're bringing it home."

"It's surreal," said Marchand. "I don't know if it will ever kick in." Marchand is a rookie. He is from Hammond Plains, Nova Scotia. He is 23 years old. How could he possibly know what this moment is like for longtime Bruins fans? How could any of the champion Bruins know?

"It's unreal," said club president Cam Neely, a man who skated and suffered through some of the tough years. "You dream about a moment like this and you don't know how you're gonna feel. I'm so proud of the whole group."

"I guess there is a Santa Claus," said Jeremy Jacobs, who has owned the Bruins since 1975 and earned a reputation as the Montgomery Burns of Boston sports. No more. It's all good now. The kind folks inside Rogers Arena in Vancouver let the Bruins hang around the ice with the Cup for almost an hour after the game and played "Dirty Water" and "Tessie" over the public address system as Boston players embraced their families and friends and posed with the Cup. Too bad they didn't play "We Are the Champions." This would be a good time to call your out-of-town friends and tell them you live in a city that recently won its seventh championship in 11 years.

You live in the only hamlet that's won the Grand Slam of North › PAGE 41

A Bruins' fan hoped the Black and Gold would draw Game 4 inspiration from the loss of Nathan Horton and Marc Savard to season-ending concussions.

GAME 1
1-0

Both teams served notice in Game 1 that this would be a highly physical Stanley Cup finals, but the Bruins felt Canucks' forward Alex Burrows (above) stepped over the line when he appeared to bite Patrice Bergeron's finger during a scrum behind the Boston net at the end of the first period. Bergeron (right) gave one official a firsthand look at the mark on his finger after the altercation, which resulted in a double-minor penalty to Burrows for roughing. The Canucks' Dan Hamhuis (opposite page) forced Milan Lucic into a head-over-heels crash landing. Adding insult to injury, the Bruins lost the opener.

CCM
BAUER
save on foods
Campbell's

Bruins' goalie Tim Thomas (above) was at his acrobatic best as he sprawled to make a spectacular second-period save on Maxim Lapierre during Game 2 at Rogers Arena. Milan Lucic (right) tied the contest at 1-1, beating Canucks' goalie Roberto Luongo at 9:00 of the second period. The Bruins took a 2-1 lead on Mark Recchi's goal 2:35 later. But it wouldn't last.

The heavy hitting of the series opener continued in Game 2, including this bone-crunching first-period collision (left) between the Bruins' Dennis Seidenberg and Vancouver's Victor Oreskovich. Nothing was more painful to the Bruins than the sight of the puck sliding into an empty goal (below) courtesy of the Canucks' Alex Burrows, who dodged a suspension for his Game 1 antics and scored 11 seconds into overtime when he swept behind the net ahead of defenseman Zdeno Chara and deftly potted the winner. Bruins goalie Tim Thomas, who had come out of the crease in an attempt to break up the play, was a picture of futility trying to get back to his station.

Reebok
29

GAME 3
8-1

The NHL's crackdown this season on blindside hits and blows to the head became the focal point of Game 3 in Boston after Canucks' defenseman Aaron Rome delivered a violent first-period hit (far left) to the Bruins' Nathan Horton. Horton, who had already passed the puck when he was leveled, was left flat on his back and was taken to Massachusetts General Hospital. The Bruins won the game, 8-1, but lost Horton (concussion) for the remainder of the series. Rome, who drew a five-minute interference major and game misconduct on the play, was suspended for four games, ending his postseason as well.

RECCHI
28
VANCOUVER
bauer

GAME 3
8-1

FROM 32 · American trophies within seven years.

It is the High Renaissance of New England sports. Our duck boat tires are balding. The vaunted Patriots now stand as the Boston franchise with the longest championship drought. The Patriots, the NFL's team of the decade, haven't won a Super Bowl since way back in 2005.

The humanity!

Let the record show that the Bruins' long-awaited return to the circle of champions came on a perfect June evening, 2,500 miles across the continent from Causeway Street. A season that started in Prague ended on Game No. 107, as the Bruins became the first team in NHL history to win three Game 7s in a single spring. It was the Bruins' first Game 7 road win in their 87-year history. And it was stunning.

A seven-game series that had finger-biting, taunting, trash talk, and embellishment ended with Bruin dominance. After losing three one-goal games at Rogers Arena, the Bruins took the fight out of the locals in the finale. Vancouver's only fight was demonstrated by nitwits who rioted after the game — fires raged and tear gas was released, giving the city another black eye.

The Bruins were inspired by the presence of Nathan Horton, who scored the game-winner in both of Boston's first two Game 7s, then was felled by Aaron Rome's late hit in Game 3 of the Stanley Cup finals. Horton splashed some Boston water on the Vancouver ice for good luck long before the start of the deciding game.

"This is the chance of a lifetime to be with my teammates," he said afterward. "I couldn't miss this."

The Canucks were strong at the jump, and with 5½ minutes left in the first period, the Bruins lost a faceoff in the Vancouver zone, but Marchand got the puck. The Ball Of Hate controlled it nicely, and centered the puck to Bergeron, who one-timed it past Roberto Luongo. Good omen. The team that scored first won every game of the finals.

Late in the second, Zdeno Chara made a crucial save. That's right. Save. After giving up the puck right in front of the Bruins' net, he assumed the goalie duties when Thomas was faked out of position. Looking like a treetop Gump Worsley, Chara stopped Alex Burrows's shot with his left knee. Nice save for the big guy.

With 7:47 left in the second, Marchand made it 2-0 on a wraparound at the left post. Once again, tire-pumpin' Luongo was not agile enough to stop the puck.

Then the Bruins struck with a shorthanded goal — the clincher. With Chara off for interference (first penalty of the night), Bergeron found himself on a shorthanded partial breakaway. As he was dragged down by Christian Ehrhoff (chasing with Alex Edler), Bergeron somehow steered the puck past the shell-shocked Luongo. The goal was reviewed and when it was announced that the goal would count, it sounded like 18,860 were taking their college boards. The Bruins had three goals on only 13 shots. Both Sedins were on the ice for all three scores. At that juncture, Luongo had whiffed on six of the last 21 shots on net.

Back in Boston, the countdown was underway. Marchand potted an empty-netter with 2:44 left. Claude Julien made sure Mark Recchi was on the ice at the end.

To the finish, Thomas remained in full Battlefly, wielding his Reebok war club like Russell Crowe in "Gladiator." Kevin Bieksa fired the puck the length of the ice as the whistle sounded. Perfect. Thomas had the puck and the Bruins had the Cup.

As for the other goalie? Here's the new joke in British Columbia:

Q: What time is it in Vancouver?

A: It's 20 past Luongo.

Actually, it was party time for the Boston contingent on the Rogers Arena ice.

At 10:52 (Boston time), the Cup appeared and NHL commissioner Gary Bettman beckoned Chara. The captain skated toward the commissioner, hoisted the chalice, skated in a circle, then presented it to 43-year-old Recchi.

Recchi had just played his last game. The veteran forward took his turn, then passed the Cup to Bergeron, who relayed it to Thomas. On and on it went. They're probably still passing it to one another as you read this.

Defenseman Andrew Alberts (opposite page) and the rest of the Canucks were helpless to stop the barrage of Bruins' goals that followed Nathan Horton's injury. Alberts, a Boston College product and former Bruin, had to look away as his ex-teammates celebrated Mark Recchi's third-period goal. The game was scoreless when Horton was carried off the ice at 5:07 of the first period, and though they failed to capitalize on their five-minute power play, the Bruins scored four unanswered goals in the second period and found the back of the net four more times in the third for a runaway victory that cut their series deficit to 2-1.

GAME 4
4-0

Game 4 at TD Garden was a tale of two goalies. A frustrated Roberto Luongo (above) was pulled from the game after allowing Rich Peverley's third-period goal (right) to close the scoring in the Bruins' 4-0 victory, while Tim Thomas (far right) made his triumphant exit at game's end with a magnificent 38-save shutout. The Bruins and Canucks were even at two games apiece and headed back to Vancouver.

THOMAS
30
11K Reebok

1K Reebok
Reebok
Reebok

GAME 5
1-0

The Bruins had exploded for 12 goals in their two victories in Boston, but drew blanks in Vancouver while Maxim Lapierre managed to beat goalie Tim Thomas at 4:35 of the third period with the lone tally of Game 5. Despite being outscored, 12-1, in their two series losses, the Canucks' dramatic victory gave them a 3-2 series lead, with all three of their wins secured at Rogers Arena by one-goal margins.

GAME 6
5-2

The Bruins continued to make life in Boston miserable for Vancouver goalie Roberto Luongo, who was removed from Game 6 after allowing three goals on the first eight shots. Luongo, who was also replaced in Game 3 at TD Garden, yielded goals (left deck, top to bottom) to Brad Marchand, Milan Lucic, and Andrew Ference before backup Cory Schneider was beaten by Michael Ryder for the Bruins' fourth goal of the period, setting a record for fastest four goals in finals history. In a familiar series scene (right), things got testy in the third period with the Canucks' Kevin Bieksa getting the worst of this scrum.

VANCOUVER
Reebok
BAUER
63

BAUER
BRUINS
46
VANCOUVER
35
Reebok
Reebok
WARRIOR
VAUGHN
VAUGHN

GAME 6
5-2

David Krejci's third-period goal past Cory Schneider (left) capped the scoring for the Bruins in their 5-2 victory in Game 6, setting up a seventh and deciding game. As was the case throughout the series, the hitting was intense, as Shawn Thornton discovered firsthand (below) while being sandwiched into the boards by Vancouver's Sedin brothers, Henrik and Daniel.

GAME 6
5-2

Working with an early four-goal cushion, Bruins' goalie Tim Thomas was his usual brilliant self, denying the Canucks a chance to climb back into the contest. Thomas made 36 stops, including this second-period gem off the stick of Vancouver winger Victor Oreskovich.

30
VAUGHN
VAUGHN

Reebok
BAUER
BOSTON
37
BAUER
28
RECCH

GAME 7
4-0

Patrice Bergeron (37) was a picture of joy celebrating his first-period goal with teammates Brad Marchand and Mark Recchi. Bergeron's goal opened the Game 7 scoring at 14:37, and he added a shorthanded goal in the second period to give the Bruins a commanding 3-0 lead. Bergeron's performance capped a stellar individual postseason, which was very much in doubt some five weeks earlier when he suffered a concussion in the Eastern Conference semifinals against Philadelphia.

The list of Canucks who turned in disappointing performances in the series was lengthy, but Roberto Luongo's name fell squarely at the top. Luongo, who was roughed up early and often in the Bruins' three victories in Boston, could do little to stem the tide in Game 7 at Rogers Arena. He was subjected to the sight of Brad Marchand's victory leap (right) into the waiting arms of Zdeno Chara following his second-period goal to give the Bruins a 2-0 lead. Marchand added a third-period empty-netter for good measure moments before Luongo made his painful exit from the ice (above) at game's end.

63
BAUER
EASTON

GAME 7
4-0

Nathan Horton (below), such an integral part of the Bruins' magical postseason march before a concussion ended his season in Game 3 of the Stanley Cup finals, was all smiles as he joined teammates Adam McQuaid (54) and Tyler Seguin for a post-game celebration. Tim Thomas (right) gave Patrice Bergeron a king-sized victory hug after posting his second shutout of the series to cap a brilliant postseason that earned him the Conn Smythe Trophy as playoff MVP. Thomas allowed the high-powered Canucks' offense just eight goals in seven games, stopping all 37 shots in the grand finale.

BOSTON
46
20

STANLEY CUP
20 11
CHAMPIONS
FINAL
Reebok
BAUER
BOSTON
23
KREJCI

GAME 7
4-0

The first of many Bruins' celebrations occurred on the Rogers Arena ice (left) following their 4-0 victory in Game 7. Canucks' diehards Sully and Force (top right), suited up in their familiar full-bodied green costumes, displayed sportsmanship in congratulating Bruins left wing and Vancouver native son Milan Lucic for his part in spoiling their dreams. Lucic took his turn hoisting the Stanley Cup (middle), much to the delight of a pair of Bruins' fans (bottom).

Zdeno Chara and Shane Hnidy were front and center during the bubbly celebration in the visitors' locker room at Rogers Arena. Back home, fans at the Bleacher Bar (below) were also in a partying mood.

Johnny Boychuk opened a bottle of beer the old-fashioned way — with his teeth — and Patrice Bergeron (left) wielded a champagne bottle. Fans spilled into Boston's Kenmore Square (below).

Patrice Bergeron's reaction to holding the Stanley Cup was a common one. He held the championship trophy over his head and planted a king-sized kiss on it as he skated around the Rogers Arena ice.

VERSUS TAMPA BAY

ELECTRICITY

The Bruins played some ragged hockey, and no lead seemed safe with St. Louis & Company buzzing. But they saved their backchecking best for last with a complete team effort in a 1-0 Game 7 classic.

LIGHTNING ■ BRUINS

Game 1

5-2

TB	3	0	2	5
BOS	1	0	1	2

SATURDAY, MAY 14, 2011 • **BOSTON**

Game 2

6-5

TB	2	1	2	5
BOS	1	5	0	6

TUESDAY, MAY 17, 2011 • **BOSTON**

Game 3

2-0

BOS	1	0	1	2
TB	0	0	0	0

THURSDAY, MAY 19, 2011 • **TAMPA BAY**

Game 4

5-3

BOS	3	0	0	3
TB	0	3	2	5

SATURDAY, MAY 21, 2011 • **TAMPA BAY**

Game 5

3-1

TB	1	0	0	1
BOS	0	2	1	3

MONDAY, MAY 23, 2011 • **BOSTON**

Game 6

5-4

BOS	2	0	2	4
TB	1	2	2	5

WEDNESDAY, MAY 25, 2011 • **TAMPA BAY**

Game 7

1-0

TB	0	0	0	0
BOS	0	0	1	1

FRIDAY, MAY 27, 2011 • **BOSTON**

BAUER
19
SEGUIN

May 28, 2011 • BOB RYAN / Globe Staff

ROUND 3

Sixty minutes. One goal. That's all Tim Thomas needed. It was 60 minutes of clean, breathtaking, exquisite hockey in the most important game of the year. It was a Game 7 for the ages, and with their 1-0 victory over the Tampa Bay Lightning, the Boston Bruins advanced to the Stanley Cup finals for the first time since 1990.

The Lightning made the Bruins work for this win until the final seconds. How closely matched were these teams, who each had finished with 103 points during the regular season? Well, they each scored 21 goals in this series. Does that tell you anything? "We had nothing left," said Tampa Bay coach Guy Boucher. "Nothing left in the tank." There was a certain irony in this outcome, since this was the second 1-0 Game 7 in which the Lightning were involved this year. That's the score by which they completed a comeback from a 3-1 first-round series deficit against the Pittsburgh Penguins.

This one turned Boston's way when Nathan Horton took a left-to-right feed from David Krejci and slipped it into the net at 12:27 of the third period, thus setting off an agonizing finish during which the delirious sellout crowd of 17,565 made more and more noise until the final horn. I don't think I've ever heard this second version of the Boston Garden rock to this extent. Some in attendance have been waiting a very long time for something this good to happen involving their beloved Boston Bruins. Few have been treated to a better game of hockey.

There's nothing in sport quite like Stanley Cup hockey, especially Stanley Cup overtime, when one teeny-weeny mistake can lead to disaster and the end of a season. Wait, this wasn't overtime? Tell it to the principals. "It felt like overtime the whole game," Boucher confessed. This was not just a game of clean, breathtaking, exquisite hockey. It was a game of clean, breathtaking, exquisite, and penalty-free hockey. That's correct. Neither referee Dan O'Halloran nor referee Stephen Walkom saw the need to raise his right hand to signify an infraction. That's because no player wished to be the guy whose borderline tripping, slashing, boarding, interference, holding the stick, or any other kind of penalty would lead to a damaging power play. If this meant there was less hitting than one might expect, so be it. Roughing? Are you mad? Not in this game.

"It was a credit to both teams' discipline and attention to detail," Boucher said. "I think the referees tonight let the two teams decide the outcome," declared Bruins mentor Claude Julien. "I thought the referees handled themselves extremely well."

Now about that Thomas fellow. He was good to very good on a night › PAGE 69

Nathan Horton (left) and Tim Thomas, heroes in the first two rounds of the playoffs, did it again in Game 7 against Tampa.

ACHUSETTS
THOMPSON
44
30
55
PURCELL
16
BAUER
BRUINS

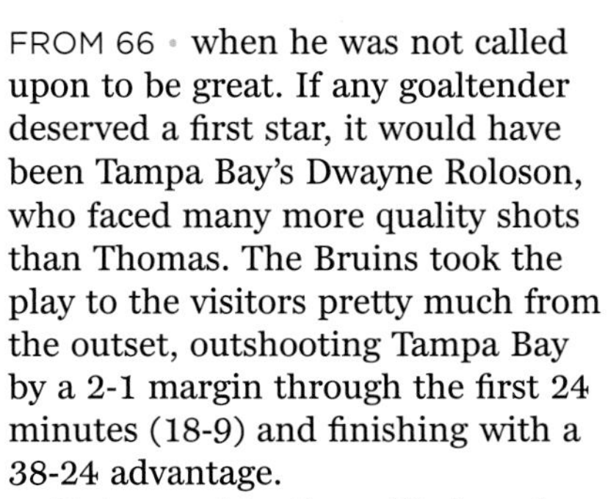

FROM 66 • when he was not called upon to be great. If any goaltender deserved a first star, it would have been Tampa Bay's Dwayne Roloson, who faced many more quality shots than Thomas. The Bruins took the play to the visitors pretty much from the outset, outshooting Tampa Bay by a 2-1 margin through the first 24 minutes (18-9) and finishing with a 38-24 advantage.

But a combination of Roloson's excellence and the Bruins' inability to finish kept the game scoreless more than 12 minutes into the third period, until Andrew Ference sprung Krejci along the left boards. Krejci deftly slid the puck to Horton, a professional goal scorer who had stationed himself where a goal scorer ought to be. The pass was perfect and the finish was perfunctory. Horton gets the goal and more of the glory, but this play was approximately 80 percent pass and 20 percent finish.

What's significant in all this is that it was the first line that got the job done. There have been times in these playoffs when Milan Lucic, Krejci, and Horton have been criticized for pulling a long-term disappearing act. So give Messrs. Horton and Krejci the requisite props for producing the biggest goal of the year.

Who would have envisioned a trip to the Stanley Cup finals when the Bruins dropped the first two games of the first-round series with Montreal? But they have talked themselves up as a "resilient" team, and now they have walked the walk, winning four of the last five from the Canadiens, sweeping Philadelphia, and then winning the two games they needed in this series after suffering an embarrassing loss in Game 4, when they were unable to hold a 3-0 lead.

They proved to their fans that they are a far different and better team than the one that lost the final four games of last year's Philadelphia series, led by a 37-year-old goaltender who had lost his job to Tuukka Rask at this time last year. Remember the moaning about Tim Thomas being an overpaid backup? I'm sure he does.

The Bruins knew Thomas would come up as big as he needed to in Game 7 against the Lightning, but they also knew it would be a lot easier on him if they avoided silly turnovers. If Tampa Bay had an odd-man rush, I can't recall it.

And they were never better than in the final seven minutes. "They played great," said Tampa Bay's Vincent Lecavalier. "Once they went up, 1-0, they really came back with those five guys, and it was tough to get anything. We got a few shots, but it was tough to get those rebounds. They really came back, tight, and as a team."

The Bruins were so persistent, the Lightning could barely get Roloson off the ice to get the sixth attacker involved. His first move to the bench with 45 seconds left lasted a second, due to a faceoff. When he was finally able to leave for good, there were only 30.2 seconds left, and it was too late to make a difference.

Sixty minutes. One goal. Now that's a proper Game 7.

GAME 1
5-2

The conference finals didn't get off to a good start for the Bruins. Tim Thomas was under siege for much of the game, including a first-period goal by Brett Clark (not pictured) that gave Tampa Bay's Teddy Purcell and Nate Thompson reason to celebrate. At the other end, goalie Dwayne Roloson (above) was the true backbone of the Lightning's solid defensive effort, stopping 31 shots in a 5-2 victory at TD Garden.

REBELL

GAME 2
6-5

Youth was served when the Bruins unleashed the offensive skills of Tyler Seguin en route to a series-tying victory. After 11 healthy postseason scratches and just 10 minutes of playing time in the opener, the Bruins' rookie exploded for two goals and two assists in the second period, including the game-tying goal 48 seconds after the puck was dropped. The Bruins finished the period ahead, 6-3, but had to hang on for dear life.

GAME 2
6-5

Game 2 hero Tyler Seguin (left) was in a giving mood following his breakout playoff appearance at TD Garden, offering a young fan the stick that produced two goals in the Bruins' 6-5 victory. Tim Thomas (right) sprawled to make this second-period save, and in the third period removed his mask to reveal a cut on his face as he disputed the Lightning's fifth goal. One of Seguin's four points in the contest came via Michael Ryder's second-period goal (bottom right), which gave the Bruins a seemingly commanding 6-3 lead. They wound up needing all of that cushion to survive a Tampa Bay comeback.

VAUGHN
VAUGHN
VAUGHN
30
Reebok

BRUINS
BOSTON

EST 1924
HOCKEY
bauer
19
SEGUIN
WARRIOR

GAME 3
2-0

Dwayne Roloson had that helpless appearance as he and defenseman Mike Lundin watched Andrew Ference's third-period shot slowly slide past the goal line with Chris Kelly on the doorstep. Kelly and his teammates celebrated the goal, which gave the Bruins insurance en route to a 2-0 victory in Tampa. David Krejci also scored for the Bruins, while Tim Thomas made 31 stops to record the shutout. It was the first game back for Patrice Bergeron, who suffered a concussion in Game 4 of the previous series.

39
39

HEDMAN
77
MOORE
19

GAME 4
5-3

The Lightning saluted the St. Pete Times Forum fans following their 5-3 victory in Game 4, which evened the series. Tampa Bay goalie Dwayne Roloson was roughed up for three first-period goals, but was one of the first to congratulate backup Mike Smith, who shut the door on the Bruins thereafter while his teammates scored five unanswered goals. Tampa Bay's stunning comeback began at 6:55 of the second period (below) when Teddy Purcell got the first of his two goals past Tim Thomas, assisted by Simon Gagne (12) with Ryan Malone (6) stationed at the post in case of a rebound.

Stick save and a beauty! The stick of goalie Tim Thomas was all that separated a shot by Steve Downie from tying the game with Dominic Moore bearing down on defenseman Dennis Seidenberg and the open goal crease in the third period of Game 5, won by the Bruins, 3-1. Of all the incredible saves made by Thomas throughout the playoffs, this one would be remembered as his defining moment. Some called it the NHL's "save of the year."

44
19
MOORE

GAME 5
3-1

Game 5 was as physical as it was dramatic, with Lightning star Steven Stamkos sent flying over Bruins' goalie Tim Thomas into the net during first-period action. Eric Brewer (bottom left) delivered a third-period hit that knocked the Bruins' Patrice Bergeron to the ice in front of Vancouver goalie Mike Smith. Offense was hard to come by, with Brad Marchand's second-period goal (top right) breaking a 1-1 tie, and Rich Peverley's empty-netter putting the finishing touches on the victory, which gave the Bruins a 3-2 series lead. No surprise that the night ended an eruption of fisticuffs (bottom right) after time ran out.

26
Reebok
CLARK
7
65
9

GAME 6
5-4

The Bruins were on the wrong end of both the scoreboard and a massive shower of noisemakers tossed from the crowd onto the St. Pete Times Forum ice following the Lightning's 5-4 victory in Game 6. Teddy Purcell and Martin St. Louis each scored a pair of goals for Tampa Bay to offset a hat trick by the Bruins' red-hot David Krejci that gave him 10 goals for the postseason. A return trip to Boston for Game 7 was next up on the itinerary for the evenly matched Eastern Conference finalists.

BAUER

GAME 7
1-0

Nathan Horton came up as big as ever at 12:27 of the third period, firing the puck past Dwayne Roloson to give the Bruins a 1-0 lead. It was the only goal of Game 7, and would not have been nearly enough to send the Bruins to their first Stanley Cup finals in 21 years if not for the supreme efforts of Tim Thomas, who stopped 24 Tampa Bay shots to record his second shutout of the series.

BOSTON
BRUINS
ROLOSON
35
WARRIOR

Tim Thomas was congratulated by his current teammates and by a former teammate at the University of Vermont, Tampa's Martin St. Louis, after the Bruins won the Eastern Conference title.

Reebok
Reebok
VAUGHN
BAUER

OLD
IME
OCKEY
BOSTON
BRUINS
Winter
CLASSIC

BOB RYAN / Globe Staff

THE FANS DEEP ROOTS KEPT US ROOTING

The Old Guy was patient. The Old Guy knew you'd come around.

Yup, Old Man Hockey knew that deep down in your heart, lodged in the depth of your psyche, there resided a little round rubber disk, right next to that little white ball with the red stitches. Football and basketball have had their moments of glory during the past two decades, but Old Man Hockey knew that the two sports permanently embedded in the local DNA were baseball and, yes, hockey.

Old Man Hockey watched in sadness as other sports elbowed him to the side. But he had faith. He knew you just needed an excuse to reacquaint yourself with a sport that has extremely deep roots in these here parts.

And you have. It has been 21 years since the Boston Bruins have even played for the Cup, and it has been 39 years since they actually won it. So much has changed, on and off the ice. Bobby Orr and Phil Esposito are in their 60s. Even Ray Bourque has hit 50.

There was no music blaring in the Old Garden, and not much in the way of video, either. There was just John Kiley, bringing the Bruins out to "Paree" and rousing the crowd during languid moments with such tunes as "Mexican Hat Dance."

When Johnny "Chief" Bucyk skated around the Garden with Lord Stanley's Cup held aloft following that 1970 triumph, there may have been six people sporting Bruins garb. This time, at least 75 percent of the playoff crowds breaking every decibel record in the newer building were wearing something black and gold, none of it cheap. Being a fan now calls for a far more substantial financial commitment than it did in Ye Olden Days. And we're not even talking about the price of tickets.

The teams are surely different. The last Bruins team to win a Stanley Cup was led by a pair of extraordinary all-time talents who played a far different game. Phil Esposito led the league with 133 points (which sounded good until Wayne Gretzky came along). The incomparable Bobby Orr augmented his annual Norris Trophy with 117 points. The Chief, who played the regular season at a spry 36, had 83. Six other Bruins had more than 50 points.

That kind of firepower doesn't exist anymore, anywhere. Milan Lucic was this team's only 30-goal scorer, sharing the team scoring lead at a rather modest 62 points with David Krejci. Patrice Bergeron had 57 points. Nathan Horton had 53. So much for 50-point men.

But these guys know how to D-up, as we say in basketball. The Bruins led the Eastern Conference in fewest goals allowed with 195, and that's the way coach Claude Julien likes it. The 1-0 Game 7 conquest of Tampa Bay represented Julien hockey at its finest. The top-to-bottom attention to detail was extraordinary. There were no sloppy passes, no careless puckhandling, and no letdown in forechecking.

The last Bruins team to win a Stanley Cup was easy enough to like, consisting, as it did, of so many A students. But this bunch is lovable more for its collective strength and its downright vulnerability than for its stars.

Well, yes, there is a star aside from Thomas. It's hard not to notice Zdeno Chara. The 6-foot-9-inch Slovakian plays about 7-4 when you throw in his skates and his stick, which enables him to execute poke checks when the play has emanated from Downtown Crossing.

It is a team with little margin for error, and it arrived in the Cup finals with a large stain on its résumé. Most teams love power plays. Some thrive on them. The Bruins would be better off if they could adopt a football policy and refuse penalties.

But Bruins fans have learned to love them despite their flaws because the game they are playing is hockey and certain elements remain constant, especially in the Stanley Cup playoffs. Your father loved hockey, and so did his father, and maybe even his father.

Detroit fancies itself "Hockeytown"? What a laugh. There is only one "Hockeytown" in America, one town where the NHL has been going on since 1924, one town where high school hockey has an eight-decade tradition, one town where you can stage an annual college hockey tournament featuring four high-quality teams within a 2-mile radius.

The Bruins are right in the center of this hockey consciousness, and have been since the '20s. The first great NHL superstar was Eddie Shore, and guess where he played all those years? We had the great "Kraut Line," champs just before WWII, and, of course, we had the Big Bad Bruins. We had Ray Bourque and Cam Neely.

Granted, it has been a frustrating 21 years for Bruins devotees. There has been a lot of teasing, and little fulfillment, since the 1992 team advanced to the conference finals, only to be slapped around by the mighty Penguins. Only a year ago, the Bruins suffered the most humiliating series loss in NHL history.

> DETROIT FANCIES ITSELF "HOCKEYTOWN"? WHAT A LAUGH.

But you knew there was something good going on when this team pulled off a 6-0 road trip from February 17 through March 1. That told you this team had an inner resolve other recent Bruins teams lacked. They showed that resolve again after losing Games 1 and 2 at home to Montreal. And here they are, playing the game you and your forefathers have always loved with spunk and heart.

Old Man Hockey knew you'd come around. All you needed was a reason to care.

VERSUS PHILADELPHIA

REVENGE

The Bruins had waited a year for the chance to redeem themselves and their fans, and they never gave the flummoxed Flyers hope for a single victory — never mind another historic comeback — in their return engagement.

FLYERS BRUINS

Game 1

7-3

	1	2	3	T
BOS	2	3	2	7
PHI	1	1	1	3

SATURDAY, APRIL 30, 2011 • **PHILADELPHIA**

Game 2

3-2

	1	2	3	OT	T
BOS	2	0	0	1	3
PHI	2	0	0	0	2

MONDAY, MAY 2, 2011 • **PHILADELPHIA**

Game 3

5-1

	1	2	3	T
PHI	0	1	0	1
BOS	2	2	1	5

WEDNESDAY, MAY 4, 2011 • **BOSTON**

Game 4

5-1

	1	2	3	T
PHI	0	1	0	1
BOS	1	0	4	5

FRIDAY, MAY 6, 2011 • **BOSTON**

Round 2 is over. With a convincing 5-1 triumph before 17,565 enraptured followers at TD Garden, the Bruins swept the Philadelphia Flyers out of the NHL playoffs. Revenge is theirs. Retribution is theirs. Peace of mind is theirs. A year ago, the Bruins suffered the most humiliating loss in their history, blowing a 3-0 series lead and a 3-0 lead in Game 7 at home to the Flyers. One year later, they have crushed the Flyers, outscoring them by a hefty 20-7 margin. This would seem to balance the scales, would it not?

"I hope so," said Boston goaltender Tim Thomas, the team's unquestioned most valuable player in the first two rounds of the playoffs. "You keep hearing about last year, and you have to ignore it to be able to do what we just did, winning this series. But to be honest, I'm glad it's over ... because the longer that series would have went, the more talk about last year. So, I'm glad that it is put behind us as a team, and organization, and the fans. I'm glad the fans can put it behind them, too. And I'll say it, hopefully exorcising some demons."

The Bruins made the fans sweat a bit, entering the third period tied at 1-1 after a Brad Marchand giveaway had led to Kris Versteeg's tying goal at 13:22 of the second period. But the third period belonged to the home team, starting with a Johnny Boychuk blast past Flyers goalie Sergei Bobrovsky at 2:42 and ending with Daniel Paille's empty-net tap-in at 19:35, at which point the unofficial Boston sports anthem, "I'm Shipping Up to Boston," had been playing ceaselessly over the PA system for about three minutes.

The playoffs had begun on a very negative note when the Bruins dropped Games 1 and 2 at home to the hated Montreal Canadiens. At that point, history was hardly their ally. They were constantly reminded that no Bruins team had extricated itself from an 0-2 hole, and never mind the events of a year ago, a disaster whose details appear to be known by every man, woman, child, and pet in the Commonwealth. And now they have won eight of their last nine games and head to the Eastern Conference finals for the first time since 1992. This is precisely why sport is so vastly different from entertainment. You have to go out and play the game, and for the last two weeks the Bruins have been playing their best hockey of the year.

Save for that one Marchand gaffe, it was all good for the Bruins in this Game 4. They started the evening with a stop-the-presses moment by scoring an honest-to-goodness, five-on-four goal, something that hasn't happened since gas was under three bucks a gallon (well, almost). And a thing of beauty it was, too, as the puck was expertly passed from Bruin to Bruin before Milan Lucic took a pass from Nathan Horton and slipped it into a › PAGE 96

David Krejci scored in the first period of Game 1 at Philadelphia, setting the stage for a sweep.

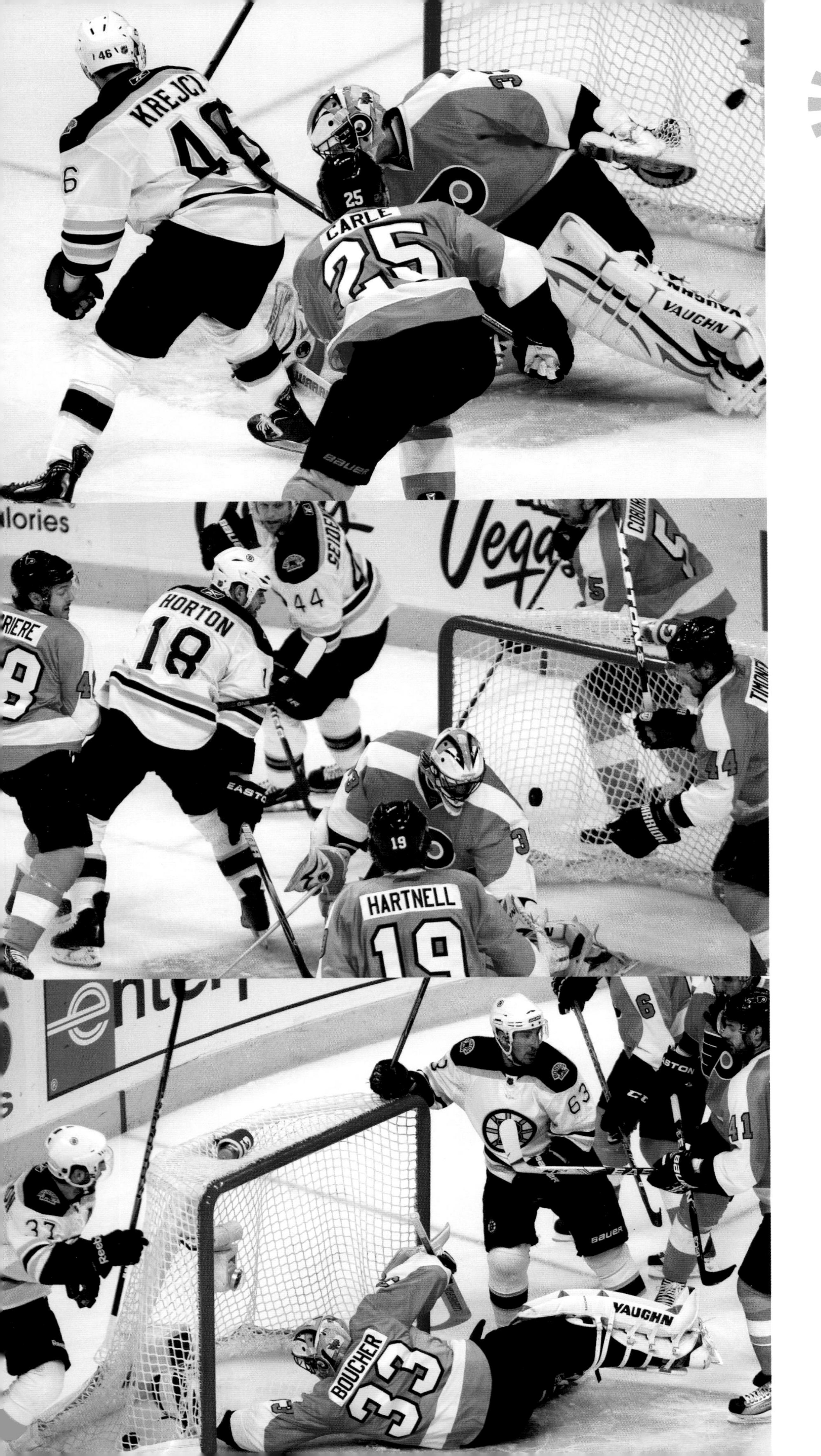

GAME 1
7-3

David Krejci's first-period backhander past Flyers' goalie Brian Boucher was the start of a goal-scoring explosion by the Bruins in Game 1. Krejci had two of the Bruins' goals in a 7-3 rout, and was joined in the scoring column by Nathan Horton, who gave his team the lead for good with his first-period goal to make it 2-1. Patrice Bergeron (left) and Brad Marchand were on the doorstep of the Flyers' net to celebrate Mark Recchi's second-period goal as the onslaught continued.

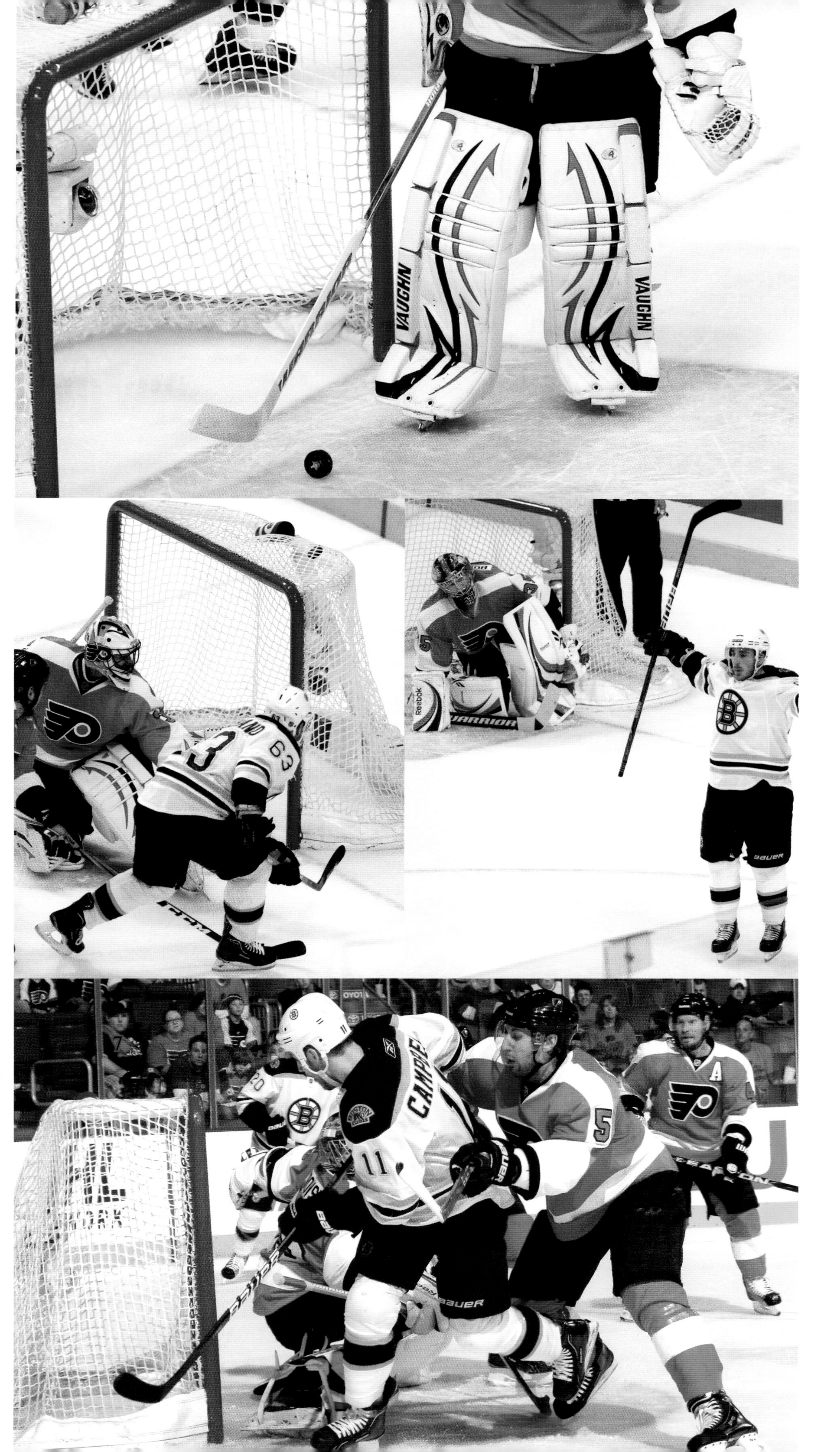

A beleaguered Brian Boucher (top) swept the puck out of the net following David Krejci's second goal. Things got worse for Boucher, who was helpless to stop the first of Brad Marchand's goals before being replaced in net by Sergei Bobrovsky. The new Flyers' goalie didn't fare much better, watching Marchand celebrate his third-period goal (middle right) before allowing Gregory Campbell's shot to sneak by (bottom), closing the scoring.

"WITH FIVE MINUTES LEFT, I LET MYSELF ... START TO THINK, 'HEY, THIS COULD BE IT; WE COULD WIN THIS GAME.' "

FROM 92 • nice 3-foot gap to the left of Bobrovsky at 12:02 of the first period.

Thomas was not being overly taxed. The Bruins were the clear aggressors. Halfway through the second period they had an 18-9 shots-on-goal advantage, and that doesn't begin to tell the story, as there were 10 or more bullets that whizzed either left or right of the goaltender.

But all it takes in hockey is one goof to turn things around, and that is what happened when Marchand lost the puck to Mike Richards and Versteeg made it 1-1 at the conclusion of the ensuing two-on-one rush with a nice move on Thomas, who really had no chance.

You can imagine the fan angst as the third period began. Losing this game would have been intolerable. But Boychuk relieved the pressure with a mighty blast that sailed over Bobrovsky's left shoulder.

"When it went in I felt relieved," said the 27-year old defenseman, whose shot is second on the Bruins only to Zdeno Chara's in terms of velocity. "The forward was coming at me very hard. I just shot a knuckler."

Watching from the other end of the ice was one very grateful goaltender.

"I was very happy, but I tried not to get too high because there was a lot of time left," Thomas said. "I didn't want to have that exhilaration, and then that crash."

The dam-burster came with a tick or two more than five minutes remaining. This time, it was Philadelphia's turn to lose the puck. Matt Carle gave it away to Horton, who has come alive at the most propitious juncture of the season. He held the puck, waited for Lucic to get a head of steam, slipped the puck to the rugged forward, and watched as Lucic sent one past Bobrovsky to make it 3-1.

Now Thomas could relax.

"When Looch scored the goal with five minutes left," Thomas said, "I let myself just a little start to, not celebrate, but start to think, 'Hey, this could be it; we could win this game.' "

Marchand scored an empty-netter at 18:04, if Thomas needed any more convincing.

There's a lot more hockey to come. But the Bruins can savor the fact that they annihilated a team that ruined their lives 12 months ago. Who could put a price on that?

Despite being down a game, Philadelphia fans assembled for Game 2 taunted Zdeno Chara with a reminder of Boston's epic collapse in last year's playoffs.

BOSTON
Reebok
Reebok
VAUGHN
VAUGHN

GAME 2
3-2

Bruins' goalie Tim Thomas (left) turned aside this blazing shot in overtime by Flyers' right wing Kris Versteeg in what turned out to be the most contested game of the Eastern Conference semifinals. The heavy hitting continued with Johnny Boychuk of the Bruins (top right) using the leverage of his stick and body to send Braydon Coburn hard into the boards. A happy ending took a bit of waiting as the Bruins' David Krejci (46) and teammates watched a video replay of his winning goal on the Wells Fargo Center scoreboard screen while it was under review.

GAME 2
3-2

Back in goal for the Flyers in Game 2, Brian Boucher showed improvement but was late attempting this stick save on David Krejci's shot at 14:00 of overtime. Krejci's fourth goal of the postseason lifted the Bruins to a 3-2 victory and set off a team-wide celebration on the Wells Fargo Center ice. The Bruins stunned the Philadelphia faithful by leaving town with victories in the first two games of the series.

LUCIC
17
Reebok
VAUGHN
BAUER

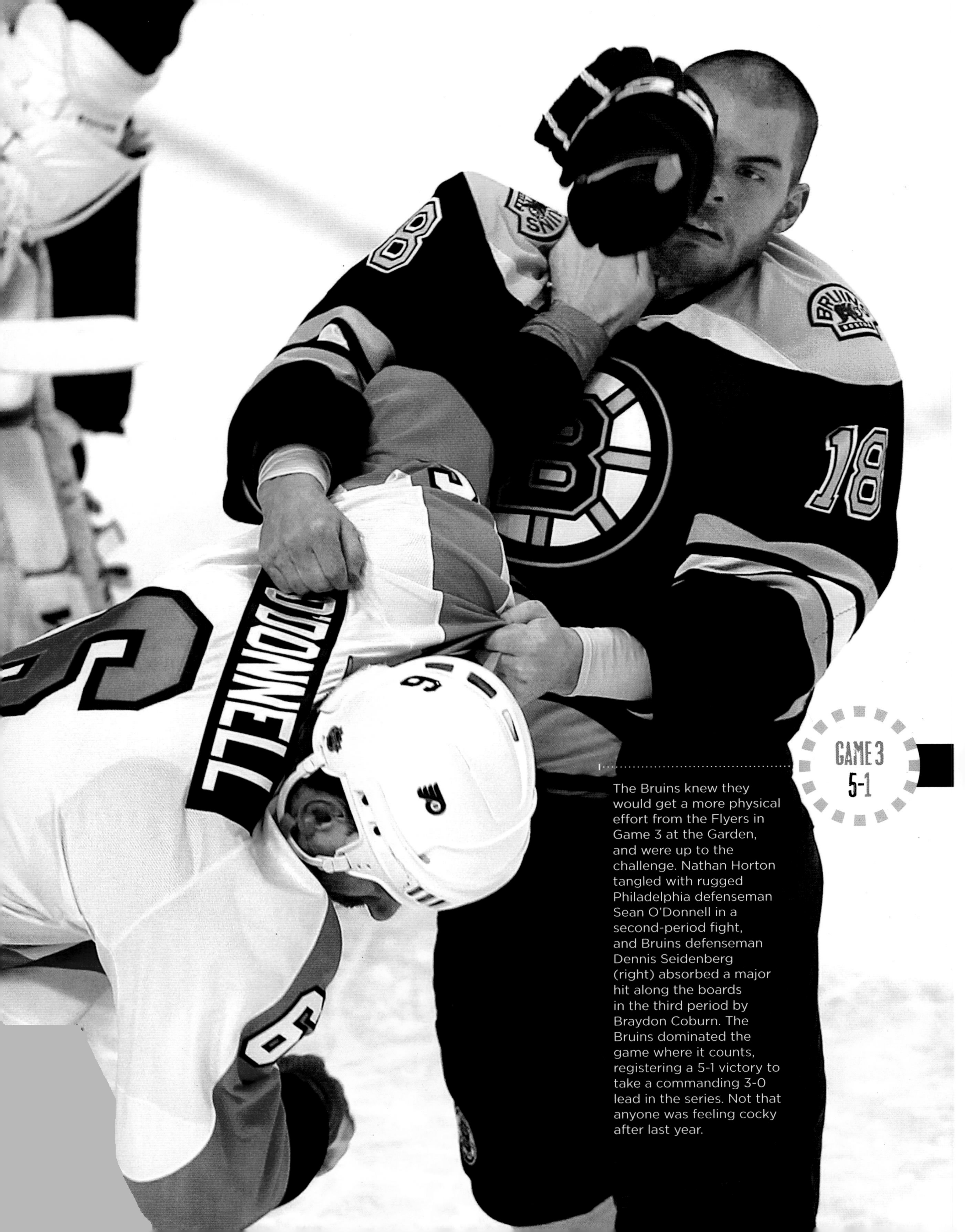

GAME 3
5-1

The Bruins knew they would get a more physical effort from the Flyers in Game 3 at the Garden, and were up to the challenge. Nathan Horton tangled with rugged Philadelphia defenseman Sean O'Donnell in a second-period fight, and Bruins defenseman Dennis Seidenberg (right) absorbed a major hit along the boards in the third period by Braydon Coburn. The Bruins dominated the game where it counts, registering a 5-1 victory to take a commanding 3-0 lead in the series. Not that anyone was feeling cocky after last year.

VAUGHN
EASTON
BAUER
BRUINS
5
44

17
Reebok

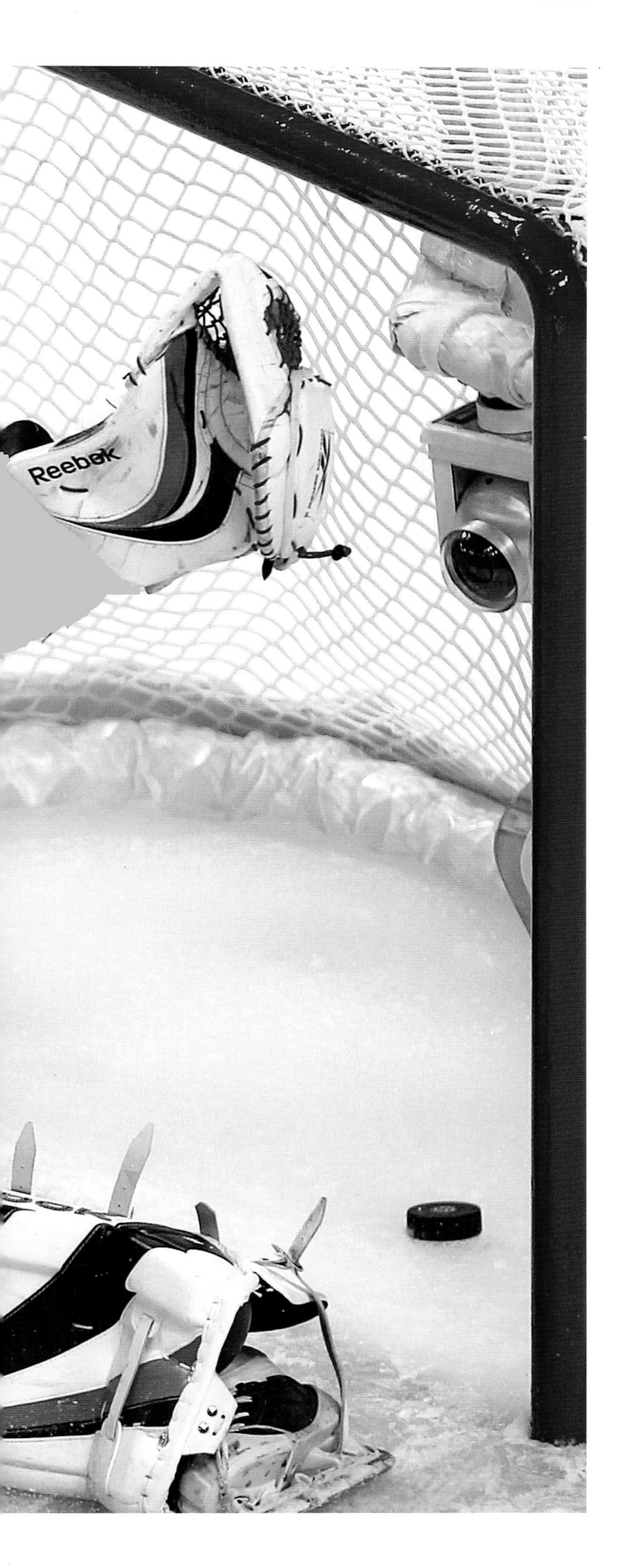

GAME 4
5-1

Milan Lucic of the Bruins was able to create space for himself in front of the Philadelphia crease before firing a shot past goalie Sergei Bobrovsky's outstretched glove hand to open the Game 4 scoring. A helpless Bobrovsky watched Rich Peverley (below) celebrate Johnny Boychuk's third-period goal at 2:42, which gave the Bruins a 2-1 lead. The floodgates opened soon thereafter, with goals by Lucic, Brad Marchand, and Daniel Paille putting the finishing touches on a 5-1 victory and series sweep.

BERGERON

GAME 4
5-1

The Bruins finished off their stunning series sweep of the Flyers with a second straight 5-1 romp, which brought smiles from coach Claude Julien and goalie Tim Thomas. But there was cause for concern regarding Patrice Bergeron (left), who had difficulty getting up from the ice following a third-period hit delivered by Claude Giroux. Bergeron did not return to the game and was diagnosed with a concussion, jeopardizing his availability for the Eastern Conference finals.

SHIRA SPRINGER / Globe Staff

JEREMY JACOBS OWNING HIS IMAGE

Sitting in the shadows of TD Garden, 20 rows from the ice, Jeremy Jacobs watched the Bruins practice for the Stanley Cup finals.

The out-of-town owner doesn't make "appearances," doesn't crave celebrity, doesn't see his role as cheerleader-in-chief. Of all Boston's major sports team owners, Jacobs, who purchased the Bruins in 1975 for $10 million, is the least visible and most restrained. Dressed in coat and tie, he spends playoff games pacing in a luxury box. The distance he keeps and the fact that his home is in East Aurora, New York, near Buffalo, largely account for his image as an aloof owner, someone too far removed from the Boston sports scene to truly value the Bruins' place in it.

Does he mind that people see him as disengaged? "That's obviously the image that I portray to them. I can't change that," said Jacobs. "... People who know me know my level of passion for my sport. Your actions have to speak louder."

Jacobs paused. "And apparently my actions haven't, my body language has sent the wrong signal. Hopefully, my body language now will change that."

Winning the NHL's ultimate prize gives the much-maligned Bruins owner a rare opportunity to remake his image. The Stanley Cup quiets longstanding critics who accuse Jacobs of caring more about the bottom line than winning, of viewing the Bruins as just another piece of his business empire, Delaware North Companies, which earns $2 billion in annual revenues from hospitality and food service.

"The image doesn't bear any relation to the real person that Jeremy Jacobs is," said NHL commissioner Gary Bettman. "No one I know is more passionate about the game of hockey and no owner more passionate about his team than he is. He is extraordinarily knowledgeable about the game and about the business of the game."

Still, Jacobs seems acutely aware of, even sensitive to, the criticism. He tries to convey the unique place the team holds in his portfolio, though sometimes it sounds like talking points more than passion.

"When you own a franchise in a city like Boston, these great, classic properties, it's not another asset," said Jacobs. "It's a civic asset that you're holding there. ... I didn't fully appreciate that until after I'd been there for several years. Then, it became more and more apparent that you were dealing with the emotions of a community and with the pride and the culture, more so than with anything else you would do."

Jacobs remains most comfortable behind the scenes, making almost daily calls to president Cam Neely and general manager Peter Chiarelli to discuss players, or solicit advice and opinions from his top executives. And sometimes to level a few quick hits with his dry sense of humor. ("He really likes to bust chops," said Neely.)

Jacobs will be the first to describe how his ownership style has "evolved," the first to acknowledge he could have handled relationships with the media better and been more available. But Jacobs came from a different school of ownership, when no one expected owners to be personalities.

"When you're dealing with a subject that you're not intimately day to day involved with, put competent people in charge and let them lead," Jacobs's father, Louis Jacobs, once told his son.

That hands-off philosophy is what Jacobs brought to the Bruins, where Harry Sinden, president of the Bruins for 17 years, was the man entrusted with the franchise. In 2006, what Jacobs calls a "watershed" year for the team, Jacobs brought in Chiarelli and Sinden moved into his senior adviser role. Coach Claude Julien and Neely arrived the next year. Jacobs said, in part, those changes were prompted by the insights of his son Charlie, who is the team's principal.

Jacobs sees the foundation for the Bruins' current success in the leadership of Neely, Chiarelli, and Julien. But he also sees something more valuable in the Bruins' current incarnation.

"I see sustainability," said Jacobs. "This community will be hockey-frenzied for the next 15 years, not just now."

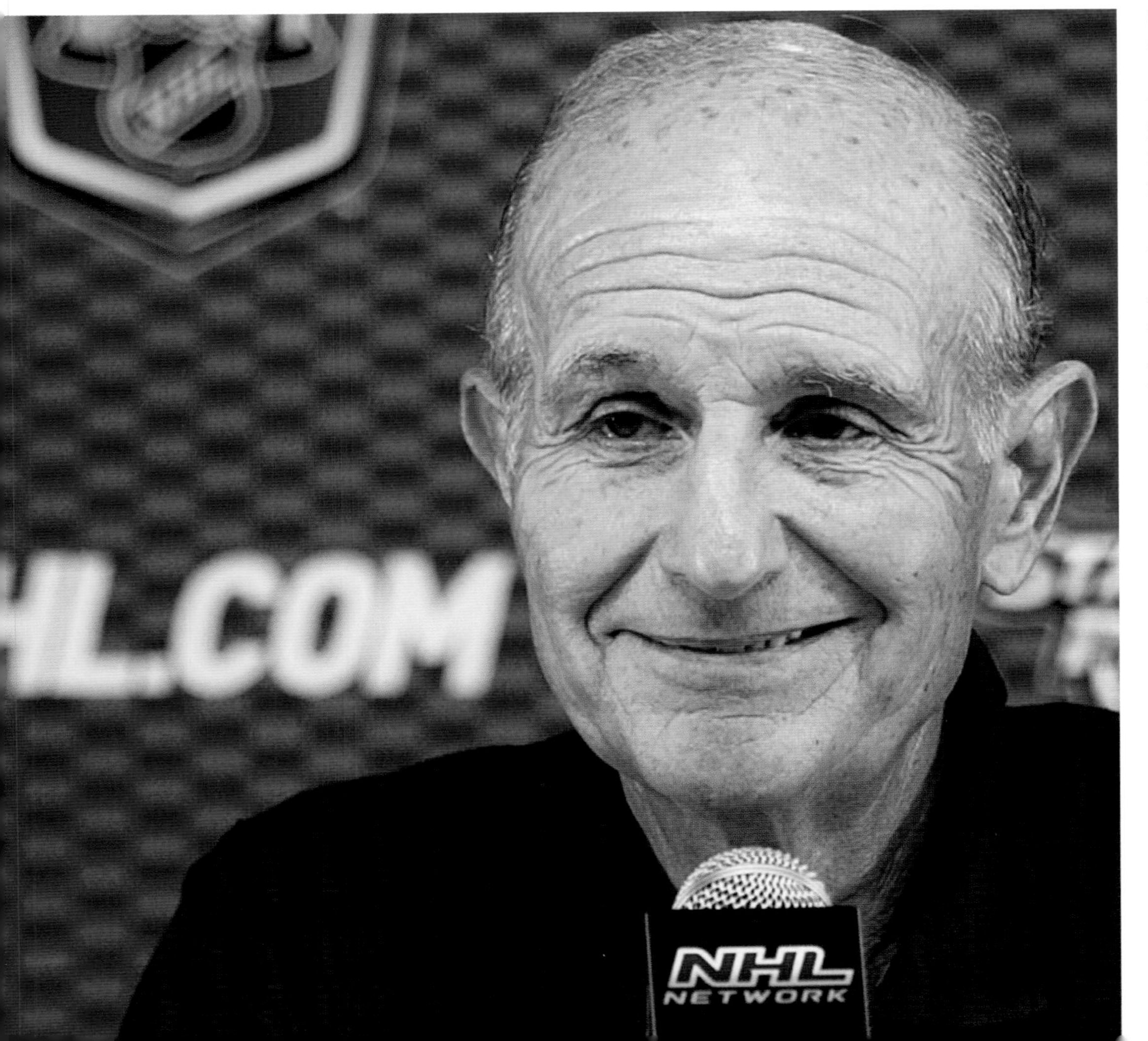

DAN SHAUGHNESSY / Globe Staff

HARRY SINDEN HOW HE SEES IT

He is 78 years old now, a great grandfather, and still a presence in the Bruins front office.

"They call me an adviser," Harry Sinden said recently when reached at his home north of Boston. "What I am is an observer. If they want, I give them my observations. Sometimes I give 'em to them even if they don't want 'em."

In more than 40 years of service with the team, as head coach, general manager, and "adviser," Sinden has always been the straightest of shooters. That has gotten him into trouble at times, and we thought maybe his bosses had locked him in the Garden basement this spring, but no. Sinden is still a vocal force in the Hub of Hockey. A few of his observations:

"I think [Tim] Thomas is the best goalie we've had since [Gerry] Cheevers. They're very similar in style. Tim is a little more athletic than Gerry. ... People ask me about him being unorthodox — how come I didn't hear those remarks about Dominik Hasek? This guy is a hell of a goalie.

"[Zdeno] Chara is just a terrific defenseman. We've had Bobby Orr and Brad Park and Raymond Bourque and now Chara. He's always one of the top two or three defensemen in the league.

"[Patrice] Bergeron is the type of player I like. He's like a Bobby Clarke or a Ronnie Francis, an all-around contributor. I like [David] Krejci, I like [Milan] Lucic. I like lots of them. They're good."

What does he think of his coach, the oft-maligned, stay-the-course Claude Julien?

"He's done a tremendous job," said Sinden. "There's a couple of aspects to coaching. You have to be able to communicate and you have to be able to get the players to play for you. He's done both of those things. These guys really want to play for him."

What about Peter Chiarelli, another guy who does a job Sinden used to do?

"We were weak at the back end of our lineup when he got here, and I think he's corrected that really well with guys like [Gregory] Campbell and [Chris] Kelly," said Sinden. "He's done a terrific job with guys like [Andrew] Ference on defense. He's supplemented this team and made it a Stanley Cup contender."

Sinden hoisted the Cup at City Hall Plaza when the Bruins were kings in 1970, but he has regrets about the near misses through the decades.

"There were disappointing times for everybody," he said. "We had a shot at winning it so many times. There was always a feeling, very much like with the Red Sox before '04. We ran up against a couple of dynasties with Edmonton, the Islanders, Montreal a couple of times."

Those near misses, coupled with Sinden's tight fiscal style, brought a big bowl of criticism to his doorstep. Looking back, he says he might do some things differently.

"It's very disappointing not to have won some championships with the teams we had, and I do have some regrets," he said. "Along with a couple of other teams in the NHL, we took on the players. We did what the league wanted us to do to prevent the lockout.

"Some teams didn't pay attention. We bore the brunt of that. We didn't sign free agents and we went to arbitration and walked away from players in arbitration. We did all the things the league wanted us to do in order to get the thing in financial order. In the end, I think we were the victims of that.

"But there are many things I would do the same. I had tremendous players. Everything starts with the players. You can talk about coaching and management and scouting, and they're all important, but it all starts with the players.

"That's why you have to give Claude Julien a lot of credit. This team has got what it takes. Do they have the same talent as the old Edmonton teams or the Islanders? Probably not. But they have that intangible. I've seen it in baseball and with the Celtics. Bobby Orr brought that kind of atmosphere here and I used to live in fear that we could lose that. Eventually, we did lose it, but this group has brought it back."

VERSUS MONTREAL

SMACKDOWN

The teams clashed for the 33d time in the playoffs (extending their NHL record), and Montreal leaped ahead, only to have the Bruins rally from an 0-2 playoff series deficit for the first time in their history.

CANADIENS ■ BRUINS

Game 1

2-0

MON	1	0	1	2
BOS	0	0	0	0

THURSDAY, APRIL 14, 2011 • **BOSTON**

Game 2

3-1

MON	2	1	0	3
BOS	0	1	0	1

SATURDAY, APRIL 16, 2011 • **BOSTON**

Game 3

4-2

BOS	2	1	1	4
MON	0	1	1	2

MONDAY, APRIL 18, 2011 • **MONTREAL**

Game 4

5-4

BOS	0	3	1	1	5
MON	1	2	1	0	4

THURSDAY, APRIL 21, 2011 • **MONTREAL**

Game 5

2-1

MON	0	0	1	0	0	1
BOS	0	0	1	0	1	2

SATURDAY, APRIL 23, 2011 • **BOSTON**

Game 6

2-1

BOS	0	1	0	1
MON	1	1	0	2

TUESDAY, APRIL 26, 2011 • **MONTREAL**

Game 7

4-3

MON	1	1	1	0	3
BOS	2	0	1	1	4

WEDNESDAY, APRIL 27, 2011 • **BOSTON**

BERGERON
37
73
28

Bruins goalie Tim Thomas (far right), was on the losing end of the game, and on the wrong end of a snow shower courtesy of Montreal's Tomas Plekanec. Thomas saved 18 of 20 shots, not good enough to offset the stellar work of his counterpart, Carey Price, who stopped all 31 Bruins' shots to record the shutout. There wasn't much for Bruins coach Claude Julien to feel good about when he looked up at the scoreboard in the closing seconds (above). Brian Gionta scored both goals for Montreal.

FROM 112 shorthanded, Canadiens defenseman Yannick Weber potted a goal on a wrist shot from the right side after Daniel Paille lost his stick — effectively making this another five-on-three goal for the Habs.

The Bruins failed to score on their 20th power play of the series at the end of the first. It had reached a point when the one-man-advantage for Boston was a decided disadvantage. You could almost see the Habs drooling at their prospects just about any time the Bruins went on the power play.

In the sixth minute of the second period, with the Bruins on the dreaded power play again, Montreal's Tomas Plekanec stole the puck from Recchi and went in alone on Boston goalie Tim Thomas. He did not miss. It was 2-2 and the Garden felt like a Temple of Doom. The Black and Gold were outshot, 12-7, in the second period.

We wondered if there was more torture in store for Bruins fans when Recchi fanned on an open net in the third. Then the Bruins struck. While Canadiens defenseman Roman Hamrlik lay on the ice, trying to sell a penalty after he was hit by Chris Kelly, the Bruins kept playing.

Andrew Ference fired a wrist shot that was blocked by Montreal goalie Carey Price, but Kelly was there for the nifty backhand rebound and a 3-2 lead with 10:16 left in the third.

The joy lasted until the final two minutes of regulation when Patrice Bergeron went off for high-sticking and Montreal defenseman P.K. Subban blasted a one-timer past Thomas for the 3-3 tie. Overtime.

Horton's slapper put the hockey universe back in order.

Neither one of these teams looked particularly Cup-worthy in this first round. The Bruins became the first team in NHL history to win a seven-game series without scoring on a power play. They will take plenty of baggage to Philadelphia.

But none of that matters. The Bruins played a Game 7 and did not choke. They sent the other guys home for the summer. Hockey lives in Boston in the spring of 2011.

In God We Trust
BRUINS
BOSTON
30
ebok

GAME 2
3-1

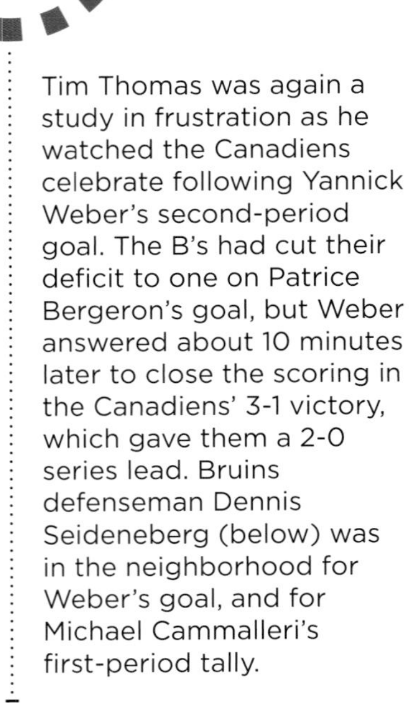

Tim Thomas was again a study in frustration as he watched the Canadiens celebrate following Yannick Weber's second-period goal. The B's had cut their deficit to one on Patrice Bergeron's goal, but Weber answered about 10 minutes later to close the scoring in the Canadiens' 3-1 victory, which gave them a 2-0 series lead. Bruins defenseman Dennis Seideneberg (below) was in the neighborhood for Weber's goal, and for Michael Cammalleri's first-period tally.

JetB
CCM
Reebok
ELLER
81
PYATT
94
68

GAME 3
4-2

Players lunging, colliding, and crashing to the ice was a familiar sight in rough-and-tumble Game 3 as the series moved to Montreal. Almost in sequence during this second-period action, Patrice Bergeron and Brad Marchand of the Bruins and the Canadiens' James Wisniewski and P.K. Subban hit the deck while pursuing the puck. The all-out effort by the Bruins produced a 4-2 victory, cutting their series deficit to 2-1.

BERGERON
37
20
WARRIOR
Reebok
BAUER

BAUER
VAUGHN
VAUGHN
VAUGHN
VAUGHN

GAME 4
5-4

Michael Ryder fired the puck past goalie Carey Price at 1:59 of overtime to give the Bruins a 5-4 victory in Game 4. Patrice Bergeron had beaten Price with a second-period goal (below), and Chris Kelly forced the overtime by notching a third-period goal (right) with just 6:18 remaining. The Bruins deadlocked the series at two games apiece, continuing an unlikely trend in which the visiting team had won every game.

GAME 5
2-1

Flanked by defensemen Dennis Seidenberg and Zdeno Chara, Bruins' goalie Tim Thomas ventured out of his crease to make this sparkling first-period save on Montreal sniper Michael Cammalleri. Game 5 also featured the obligatory Boston-Montreal dustups, including a second-period fight between the Bruins' Brad Marchand and Tomas Plekanec that was finally broken up by two referees. Nathan Horton (opposite page) eventually played the hero.

BOYCHUK
55
46
TOTALONE
BAUER

PRICE
31

GAME 5
2-1

Brad Marchand barely missed sneaking the puck past an out-of-position Carey Price in the first overtime, but the Montreal goalie was not as fortunate in the second extra session as Nathan Horton potted the game-winner (below) in the Bruins' 2-1 victory, giving them their second straight overtime victory and first series lead.

GAME 6
2-1

Milan Lucic (below) earned an escort off the ice after drawing a game misconduct on his second-period boarding penalty. Lucic's ejection was part of a frustrating night for the Bruins at Bell Centre, summed up by defenseman Zdeno Chara's expression (right) following Michael Cammalleri's goal to open the scoring for Montreal. The Canadiens' 2-1 victory forced a deciding seventh game in Boston.

ypass
33
GIONTA
21
14

EAS
EAS ON

Oh no you didn't! Montreal's Scott Gomez tries without success to knock the puck loose from the outstretched glove of Bruins' goalie Tim Thomas during the first period of Game 7. Injured Bruins' center Marc Savard (below) was inactive throughout the postseason, but had the best seat in the house for this major collision between teammate Chris Kelly and the Canadiens' Jeff Halpern.

GAME 7
4-3

It took another overtime to get the job done, but David Krejci (46) and his teammates finally got past Carey Price when Nathan Horton's goal gave the Bruins a 4-3 victory in the seventh game of their Eastern Conference quarterfinal series. Chris Kelly (top right) scored the third goal in the third period before P.K. Subban answered for the Canadiens, setting the stage for the dramatic overtime session and the celebration (bottom right) that followed.

VAUGHN
PEVERLEY

FLUTO SHINZAWA / Globe Staff

TIM THOMAS NET RESULTS

For goalies, the NHL is no place for snowflakes. It is a cookie-cutter league, now more than ever, one that prefers identical approaches over independent thinking. The preferred blueprint is that of Tuukka Rask: taller than 6 feet, flexible as Gumby, glove up, imposing even when down on his pads, most certainly playing the butterfly style.

Among that uniformity, the 5-foot-11-inch, 201-pound Tim Thomas is as unique as the white mask that protects his head (he prefers vertical bars instead of the universal cat's-eye design).

"I do play differently," said Thomas, "than just about anybody in the world."

His game, born from a battler's approach and a creative hockey mind, has made him the best goalie on Earth right now. That style, developed in six states (Michigan, Vermont, Alabama, Texas, Rhode Island, Massachusetts) and four countries (United States, Canada, Sweden, Finland), has more in common with a tornado than an efficient Swiss timepiece.

When a forward tiptoes into his crease, Thomas doesn't hesitate to chop him with his stick or step around him to get a better view of the play. If a shooter slashes into his slot, Thomas often employs a backstroke-like swim move to foil any second shot — he's assuming he'll stop the first — that might be coming. When a stray puck bobbles into his view and teammates are nowhere in sight, Thomas will go into a full swan dive to nudge it out of dangerous situations.

"Thinking outside the box," Thomas said. "I'm creative as far as finding different ways to get the job done. I might not necessarily have all the tools that other goalies have. But I'm willing to use my tools in creative ways."

In the fall of 1997, Thomas graduated from the University of Vermont and started his pro career. The hydrant-shaped goalie with the indescribable style had been selected by the Quebec Nordiques in the ninth round of the 1994 draft but was dismissed by what were then the Colorado Avalanche after his first pro training camp.

What scouts, coaches, and general managers saw was a helter-skelter scrambler. They didn't even see Thomas as having a technique. In their eyes, he was a goalie with an unheralded pedigree. To be less kind, a flopper.

Thomas disagreed. In 1997-98, while playing for HIFK Helsinki, he posted a 1.62 goals-against average and a .947 save percentage. Three years later, this time for Karpat, he had a 2.45 GAA and a .925 save percentage.

They were numbers that should have merited at least a sniff from NHL teams. But with limited viewings, scouts did not take a panoramic perspective of Thomas's performance.

"I do stuff that people don't associate with normal goaltending," he said. "It's one of my strengths. But if you're looking as a goaltending scout, I don't think they can stick their neck out to say that I'm going to be able to do it on a consistent basis. I think that's what they were saying earlier in my career."

So Thomas became a nomad. In the late 1990s, he played in Finland alongside future NHLers Olli Jokinen, Brian Rafalski, Jussi Jokinen, and Jarkko Ruutu. In 2004-05, during the NHL lockout, Brian Campbell and ex-Bruin Glen Metropolit were among Thomas's teammates.

"I have a well-rounded game," Thomas said. "I think every league I played in gave me a different discipline that I was exposed to."

In 2005-06, Thomas finally got his shot at age 31. He went 15-11-0 with a 2.26 GAA and a .923 save percentage for Scott Gordon's AHL team in Providence, then went unclaimed when he was recalled by Boston. The following season, the first under new management, Thomas went 30-29-4 with a 3.13 GAA and a .905 save percentage.

In the summer of 2007, when Dave Lewis was fired as Bruins coach after one season, Thomas had to win the confidence of a new man, Claude Julien.

"I've always been one of those guys that's said, 'As long as the goaltender stops the puck, I don't care,' I really don't," said Julien. "You can get these goaltenders that are technically sound, but they can't stop a puck.

"His compete level was there. At the same time, when I spoke to Timmy at the beginning, I said, 'My job is to make it easier on you as best I can by getting a good structure in front of you so you don't have to guess. You need to know how the players in front of you will react, which will help your style, too.'

"To me, he's been good every year. [In 2009-10] he had a good year. Not a great year. But a bit of that was the result of his health." (That season, Thomas was slowed by wear and tear in his left hip, which ultimately required surgery for a torn labrum.)

> "I DO PLAY DIFFERENTLY THAN JUST ABOUT ANYBODY IN THE WORLD."

How good could Thomas have been had his NHL chance arrived earlier? Put him in the position of Rask, who was an NHL rookie at 22 in '09. Plug in approximations of Thomas's performance, stretch them out over 15 or so seasons, and the numbers could challenge those of Martin Brodeur (612 wins, 114 shutouts).

Thomas hasn't given that much consideration. Instead, he combines his accomplishments to put his career into perspective.

"If I look back on all of those," he said, "then I think I've put together a record to be proud of personally."

Tim Thomas was never better than during the playoffs, where more than once he showed he wasn't afraid to get physical and lay it all on the line. He also took time to reflect and celebrate. In the end, he made it all look easy.

CHEERS & JEERS

Their regular season began with the two-game NHL Premiere series against the Phoenix Coyotes in Prague, and ended six months later against the Devils in New Jersey. In between, despite bumps, the Bruins served notice that the team would be a major player in the Eastern Conference in 2010-11.

OCTOBER

6-2-0

After losing the opener, Boston blanked Phoenix on the back end of the series in Prague, 3-0, beginning a four-game winning streak. They closed the month with shutout victories over Toronto and Ottawa.

JANUARY

8-4-2

New Year's Day did not result in any celebrating for the Bruins in a 7-6 shootout loss to the Sabres, but they rebounded to beat the Maple Leafs two days later, and finished the month with victories in seven of 10 games.

APRIL

3-2-0

With the playoffs on the horizon, the Bruins bested the Thrashers, Islanders, and Senators. Their loss to the Devils in the finale took nothing away from an impressive 103-point campaign.

NOVEMBER

6-6-2

Not a stellar month for the Bruins, but they still managed to record three straight victories in Eastern Conference matchups against the Devils, Rangers, and Panthers.

FEBRUARY

8-4-0

Boston's most productive month began with three straight victories and ended with five straight, the latter streak including a 3-1 victory over the Canucks in Vancouver. A sign of things to come.

DECEMBER

8-3-3

Boston began with victories over Philadelphia and Tampa Bay, the teams they would see in the Eastern Conference semifinals and finals. The Bruins also beat the Lightning later in the month as part of a Florida sweep.

MARCH

Carrying the momentum of their February winning streak, the Bruins began the month with victories over the Senators and Lightning. They slumped to lose four in a row and six of seven before rediscovering their touch with victories in four of their next five.

2010/2011 EASTERN CONFERENCE

NORTHEAST	W	L	OT	PTS
Boston	**46**	**25**	**11**	**103**
Montreal	44	30	8	96
Buffalo	43	29	10	96
Toronto	37	34	11	85
Ottawa	32	40	10	74

*The Bruins had five OT losses and six shootout losses. (Their 103-point total reflects two points for each win, plus 11 points, one for each OT or shootout loss.)

April 11, 2011 • FLUTO SHINZAWA / Globe Staff

SEASON For those who care, and they can be counted on fingers and toes, the score of the final Bruins game of the regular season was 3-2 at the Prudential Center in Newark. The rumor was that the Devils won. "Just one of those games where you're glad it's out of the way," said Bruins coach Claude Julien when it was over. His focus immediately turned to the playoffs, which once again meant squaring off with the Canadiens. No other clubs have played each other as often (33 times, and counting) in the postseason.

Two years ago, the Bruins booted the Canadiens in four games. In 2007-08, Julien's first year at the helm, the upstart Bruins engaged the Canadiens in a seven-game dogfight before bowing out in the first round. The rivalry required no further stoking. But this season, tempers flared white hot. P.K. Subban flattened Brad Marchand with an open-ice wallop December 16. On February 9, during an 8-6 Boston win, there were six fights, including a center-ice throwdown between goaltenders Tim Thomas and Carey Price.

"The hatred is definitely there again," Bruins forward Milan Lucic said. "That's what makes this game fun. That's why it's great to be part of this rivalry." The boiling point came March 8. That night at the Bell Centre, Zdeno Chara drove Max Pacioretty into a stanchion. Pacioretty was diagnosed with a fractured vertebra and a severe concussion that put him out for the rest of the season.

After Chara escaped suspension — he was tagged with an interference major and a game misconduct that night — Montreal fans went into a tizzy. They called 911, demanding Chara be cuffed and booked. The Montreal police opened an investigation. Air Canada threatened to yank its sponsorship unless the league addressed head shots.

Upon all this, Mark Recchi unleashed a steady stream of gasoline. On March 23, during a 98.5 WBZ-FM interview, Recchi hinted that the Canadiens had embellished the severity of Pacioretty's injuries in hopes of getting Chara suspended. The next day, after a 7-0 thumping of the Canadiens, Recchi said he had made his flammable comments to take the heat off his captain.

In their final game before the playoffs, the Bruins stamped a bookend on a regular season that started in Prague. They ended the year in third place in the Eastern Conference, a respectable finish given the absence of Marc Savard, their ace playmaker.

There were other positives. Rich Peverley and Chris Kelly, acquired from › PAGE 139

TOTALONE
33

CZECH MATE

10/3/10

Far away from home, the Bruins opened the season in Prague with a pair of games against the Phoenix Coyotes. Not so far away from home, Slovakian-born Bruins' captain Zdeno Chara and Czech teammate David Krejci posed in front of the NHL Premiere poster that greeted their arrival overseas. The Bruins lost the opener, 5-2, and won the second game, 3-0.

ONE TO WATCH

10/28/10

Rookie Tyler Seguin gave Bruins' fans a glimpse of his offensive skills in a 2-0 victory at TD Garden, beating Toronto goalie Jonas Gustavsson (right) for his second goal of the season. Seguin celebrated with teammates afterward.

FROM 136 • Atlanta and Ottawa, respectively, to firm up the roster, scored the Boston goals. Tim Thomas broke Dominik Hasek's all-time save percentage record. Chara placed himself in the conversation for a second Norris Trophy. Lucic busted the 30-goal mark. Brad Marchand blossomed from fourth-line energy forward to a top-six, all-around threat. For the fourth straight year under Julien, the Bruins qualified for the playoffs.

"There were a lot of things we accomplished," Julien said. "Defensively, always at the top of the league. Offensively, I think we're fifth. Our power play is the thing people have talked the most about. Hopefully we get that going in the right direction in the playoffs and it makes a difference."

"When you look at the whole season, our team was climbing and climbing and climbing. There wasn't too many times when it took a dip. Or if it did, it wasn't a long dip. It was pretty consistent, although people seem to see it a different way. You look around, there were probably a lot of teams that had bigger dips than we did. I'm trying to stay positive and look at the positive things."

His players were also looking on the bright side, and looking ahead. "The two games we won in Boston, we just played," said Lucic. "That's what we're going to have to do — play our game and skate. I think when we're moving our feet, skating well with the puck, and making plays at high speed, that's when we're most effective."

"OUR POWER PLAY IS THE THING PEOPLE HAVE TALKED THE MOST ABOUT."

HIS 15 MINUTES

10/28/10

As satisfying as it was to see the Bruins notch a 2-0 win over the Maple Leafs, the other memorable thing about this night was the fitting tribute it delivered for one of Boston's all-time hockey greats. Milt Schmidt, who was seated at center ice with members of the current team behind him during a pre-game ceremony, had a hand in raising his name and jersey number to the TD Garden rafters.

YELLOW MEN

11/15/10

Vancouver may have Sully and Force, but a pair of Bruins' fans put their own spin on the body stocking as they celebrated Michael Ryder's first-period goal behind the New Jersey bench. That was all goalie Tim Thomas needed as the Bruins went on to post a 3-0 victory at TD Garden.

LOST CONTACT LENS?

11/18/10

Milan Lucic and Nathan Horton of the Bruins have company from the Florida Panthers' Marty Reasoner and Chris Higgins as they attempt to dig out the puck along the boards during first-period action at TD Garden. The Bruins won the game easily, 4-0, behind stellar goaltending from Tuukka Rask, who made 41 saves to record the shutout.

ROUGHING

12/18/11

The Bruins' Adam McQuaid demonstrated throughout the 2010-11 season that he had no problem dropping the gloves. He went at it with Washington's Matt Bradley in a first-period fight during the Bruins' 3-2 victory, which also included an uncomfortable experience with the TD Garden glass for Milan Lucic courtesy of a check by the Capitals' John Erskine.

SHOWER CAPS

1/17/11

Doing some on-ice shopping following Zdeno Chara's hat trick to close the scoring against the Carolina Hurricanes, Bruins' goalie Tim Thomas chose a stylish one for his high-scoring teammate. Thomas had reason to celebrate himself, recording a shutout in the Bruins' 7-0 victory.

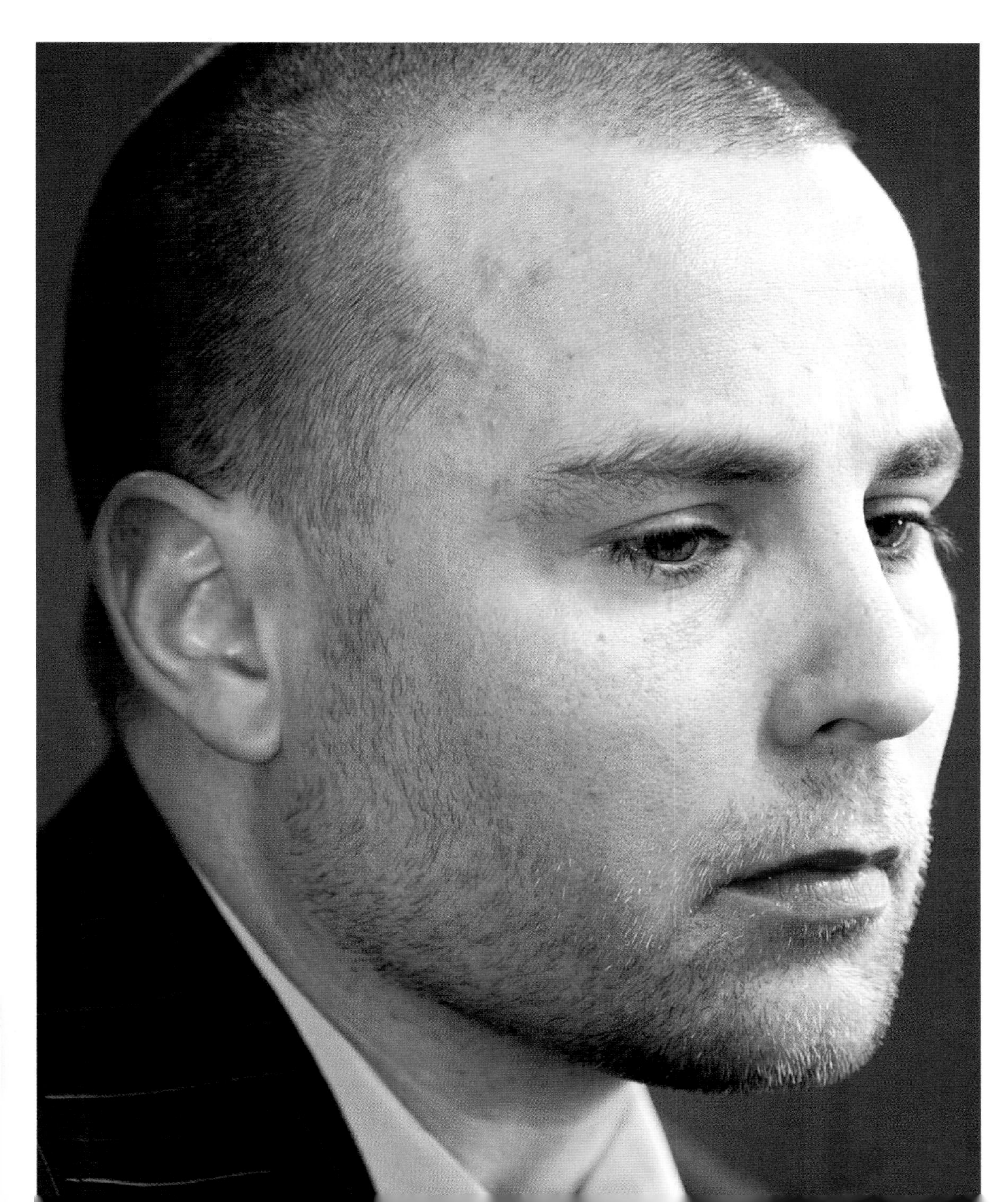

HARD DAZE

1/22/11

The Bruins' season was filled with magical moments, but also had its trials and tribulations. Marc Savard, one of the NHL's best playmaking centers, sustained his second concussion in less than a year on Jan. 22 at the hands of Colorado's Matt Hunwick. Weeks later, a forlorn Savard was left to ponder his future while sitting at a press conference on Feb. 7 in which general manager Peter Chiarelli announced he would sit out the remainder of the season.

FIGHT CLUB

2/3/11

As always, the season had a heaping helping of big-time bouts, including Andrew Ference's unanimous decision against Adam Burish (above left), and a slugfest between Gregory Campbell and Steve Ott in which goalie Tim Thomas enjoyed his ringside seat (above right). Both dustups were part of a game against Dallas at TD Garden that featured three fights in the first four seconds. Campbell's face told the story of a hard-nosed game won by the Bruins, 6-3.

'TENDER MOMENTS

2/9/11

Just six days after the Bruins and Stars waged their blood-and-guts affair, the TD Garden ice was even more violent during the archrival Canadiens' visit to town. Things got so out of hand that even goaltenders Tim Thomas and Carey Price went at it. They eventually stopped fighting, but the teams racked up an eye-popping 187 penalty minutes. And, oh by the way, the Bruins won the game, 8-6.

CUP PREVIEW

2/26/11

Not known for a physical style of play, Tomas Kaberle demonstrated he could dish out punishment every now and then. He took down Manny Malhotra of the Canucks during the Bruins' 3-1 victory in Vancouver on Feb. 26. Kaberle also contributed to the offense with an assist. Three months later, these teams would be back at it with much higher stakes involved.

POWERING UP

2/18/11

The Bruins hoped to bolster their power play when they acquired playmaking defenseman Tomas Kaberle from the Toronto Maple Leafs. Traded for the first time in his 12-year NHL career, Kaberle barely had time to get acquainted with his new teammates — other recent additions included Rich Peverley and Chris Kelly — before taking the ice in Ottawa for warm-ups.

CCM
BOSTON
12
Reebok
CCM
27

AWAY TEAM

2/17-3/1/11

The Feb. 26 win in Vancouver was part of a perfect six-game road trip that lifted the Bruins heading into March. Their run began on Feb. 17, when Islanders goalie Nathan Lawson (below) was left to watch Daniel Paille and Shawn Thornton celebrate Gregory Campbell's goal in a 6-3 victory in New York. Tomas Kaberle (right) kept a close eye on the Flames' Tim Jackman during a 3-1 victory in Calgary on Feb. 22. Milan Lucic of the Bruins and Jim Vandermeer of the Oilers (below right) traded punches in the third period of a 3-2 victory on Feb. 27 in Edmonton. In pursuit of the puck, Patrice Bergeron (far right) bowled over the Senators' Bobby Butler during the Bruins' 1-0 victory on March 1 in Ottawa, where

Boston had also won a 4-2 decision on Feb. 18. Nathan Horton celebrated with teammates (far right, bottom) after scoring the lone goal in the third period.

Reebok
BAUER
KUBA
17
54
BOSTON
WARRIOR

THE HIT

3/8/11

The hit heard around Canada came at Bell Centre as Zdeno Chara delivered a bone-crushing check on Max Pacioretty at 19:44 of the second period. The force of Chara's check sent Pacioretty headfirst into a glass stanchion, after which he lay motionless. Pacioretty suffered a concussion and fractured vertebra. Habs fans called 911 asking for a criminal investigation. Chara's sentence was a major penalty for interference and a game misconduct.

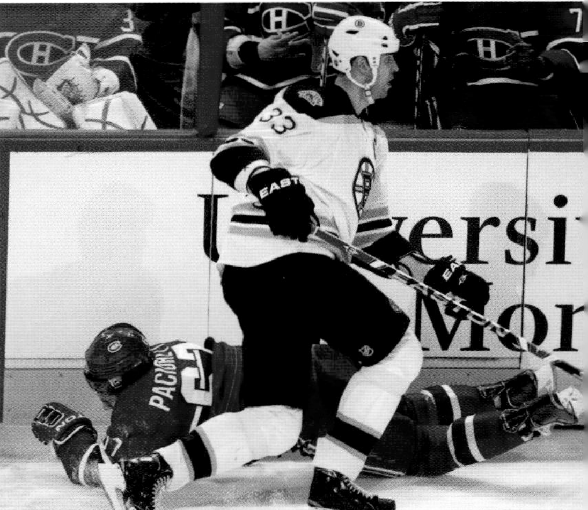

THE HIT MAN

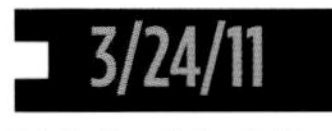

While his hit on Max Pacioretty did not result in a fine or suspension from the league, Zdeno Chara remained a wanted man in Montreal. His popularity in Boston was never in question, however, as demonstrated by the warm runway greeting he received from TD Garden fans en route to the ice before the Bruins and Canadiens met again on March 24. The Bruins won easily, 7-0.

ALISON O'LEARY / Globe Correspondent

RENE RANCOURT ANTHEM MAN

One man has started more games for the Boston Bruins than anyone else and outlasted stars like Ray Bourque and Cam Neely with his tux immaculate and nary a hair out of place. He's Rene Rancourt, a Natick, Massachusetts resident who has sung "The Star-Spangled Banner" at the opening of Bruins games for some 30 years.

Rancourt's anthem-singing in Boston actually began at Fenway Park, soon after he won an opera audition competition that was broadcast on the radio and heard by the late John Kiley, who was a longtime Boston Garden and Fenway Park organist. And the biggest event of his career also took place in Fenway, when he was called to fill in for the late singer Kate Smith, who had canceled her appearance just hours before the dramatic sixth game of the 1975 World Series between the Cincinnati Reds and the Boston Red Sox.

Nate Greenberg, assistant to Bruins president Harry Sinden, remembers that Rancourt was hired in 1976 on the strength of his voice. "We tried a couple of other people, but no one worked out very well. The problem was that the sound system in the Boston Garden was horrid, and none of them had voices that carried. ... He had a booming voice."

While he may also be heard at local youth sports events or kicking off an auto race in New Hampshire, Rancourt is in his element when the carpet is rolled onto the ice and, with opposing teams watching, he briefly steps into the spotlight.

The minute-long performances have added up over the years, until his name is readily identified with the black and gold of Boston's hockey tradition. He's the only person named in the punk rock group Dropkick Murphys' ode to Bruins games, a rollicking tune called "Time to Go."

And he notes that he'll always be part of Bruins trivia as the only national anthem singer to contribute indirectly to a player's injury, when Bruin Bob Joyce separated his shoulder tripping over the carpet placed on the ice for Rancourt.

Rancourt thrives on the thunderous applause that signals readiness for the opening puck drop of a NHL game. He puts his mark on his performances by pumping his fist at the end of the anthem, a gesture he said he picked up from Bruins player Randy Burridge. But even after 30 years of performing before huge crowds, it's still a nerve-racking challenge to sing the national anthem.

"I'm never comfortable singing it," he said. "If there's anything wrong with you, it will show in the song. I very rarely get it right, and that's why I like it. The challenge is very stimulating. There have been maybe 10 times in my career when I think I sang it really well."

"I'M NEVER COMFORTABLE SINGING IT."

Rene Rancourt has had his moments at Fenway (far left) and elsewhere. But he's best known for bringing a bit of Vegas to 30 years of singing the National Anthem before Bruins games, including the signature fist pump he picked up from former Bruin Randy Burridge.

MAKING HISTORY

GLORY DAYS

With six Stanley Cups in 18 trips to the finals, the Bruins are no strangers to the winners' circle. Their biggest stars' numbers have been retired to the Garden rafters. But many more have won our hearts, even if they never hoisted the Cup here.

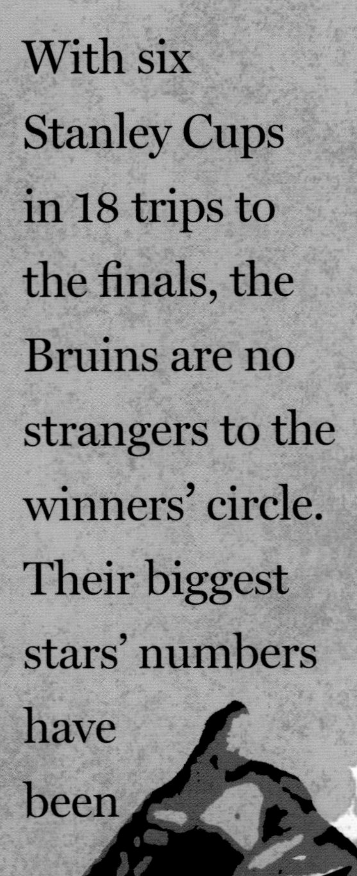

Bobby Orr was a face in the crowd when his moment of flight was immortalized with a bronze statue outside TD Garden 40 years after his Stanley Cup-winning goal.

2007/08-PRESENT

BY KEVIN PAUL DUPONT/ Globe Staff

The old Boston Garden, its sightlines steep and ideal for hockey, opened in 1928. But the Bruins were a success with the Boston sporting public even before moving into their new rink above the rumbling trains of North Station.

Owned by grocery store magnate Charles F. Adams, and with Art Ross the coach and general manager, the Boston Professional Hockey Association Inc. had routinely packed fans into Boston Arena. The Roaring Twenties were in full swing when C.F. Adams plunked down his $15,000 and bought the NHL's first American franchise. › PAGE 158

FROM 157 • Chicago, Detroit, and New York all entered in '26. The Celtics wouldn't be born for another 20-plus years when the Bruins christened the franchise against the Montreal Maroons on December 1, 1924. The Red Sox already were six years into a World Series victory drought that would last awhile. And Billy Sullivan, his Boston Patriots not born until 1960, hadn't yet learned how to dial his first lawyer.

Hockey in the Hub became instantly hot, a sport that captivated audiences with its spirited contact and its condoned — if not encouraged —brawling. Scores were low in the early days, but fists were often high. On top of it all, the Bruins were operating in the economic winter wonderland of what amounted to a sports entertainment monopoly.

There was even a night (November 15, 1927), before they moved to the Garden, when ex-Red Sox lefthander Babe Ruth sat in the Arena and watched the Bruins and Black Hawks battle to a 1-1 tie.

"Never saw anything like it," said the Bambino, treated to some ferocious hitting that evening by Bruins defenseman Eddie Shore. "Thank God I'm in baseball, with its peace and quiet."

The Bruins' early years in the Garden brought them three Stanley Cups in a little more than a decade ('29, '39 and '41). A night in the Garden to see the Bruins play then was akin somewhat to going to the theater. Men wore suits and hats. Women wore dresses. It was an occasion, an event to see the likes of Shore and Cecil "Tiny" Thompson and later the fabled "Kraut Line" —Milt Schmidt, Bobby Bauer, and Woody Dumart. It was a respectable crowd, dotted here and there with lockjawed Boston Brahmins out to see what was sometimes a nasty night of entertainment. The most loyal of the fans, the Gallery Gods, sat in the cheapest seats in the house.

They were rewarded on April 16, 1939, when the Bruins pinned a 3-1 loss on the Maple Leafs to win the first of two Cups (the other in 1970) they would seal on Causeway Street. Shore, who had retreated to the locker room after the final whistle, was summoned back by the chanting crowd. "And

Goaltender Tiny Thompson and defenseman Eddie Shore (2) led the Bruins to Stanley Cups in 1929 and 1939.

Dit Clapper, the only Bruin on three championship teams.

Goalie Frankie Brimsek clears the puck during Game 1 of the 1939 Stanley Cup finals.

All three members of the legendary "Kraut Line," (left to right) Woody Dumart, Bobby Bauer, and Milt Schmidt, are in the Hall of Fame.

1941 Mel Hill (foreground), who'd earned the nickname "Sudden Death" by scoring three overtime goals in the 1939 playoffs, helped the Bruins to another Cup two years later.

when Edward Shore skated out on to that ice," recalled Schmidt, "the ovation that man received … I can still hear it and feel it."

Shore played only four more games in a Bruins uniform after the '39 Cup win, finishing out his career in 1940. His departure followed by the start of World War II dealt the Bruins two devastating blows.

Boston netminder Frank Brimsek lost two seasons to the war. The Krauts each gave up three-plus seasons, departing en masse for the duration on February 11, 1942, one of the most memorable evenings in franchise history. The Bruins smacked around the Habs, 8-1, and the line of Schmidt, Bauer, and Dumart divvied up half of the evening's 22 points. When it was over, the Krauts were called to center ice, where they were presented with gifts and paychecks, and ultimately carried around the Garden on the shoulders of the Canadiens.

The classy Montrealers went on to win a pair of Cups by the spring of '46. The Bruins, who had won the Cup 10 months before the Krauts' departure, wouldn't win another until 1970.

"Mr. Art Ross gave us a Royal Canadian Air Force pilot's watch that night," recalled Schmidt. "To this day, I've never understood how the thing works."

The Bruins made it to the finals only once more in the '40s (a 4-1 series loss to the Canadiens in '46), and three times in the '50s (three more losses to the Canadiens in '53, '57 and '58). Following a defeat to Toronto in the '59 semifinals, Boston went a franchise-worst eight straight seasons without qualifying for the postseason.

Attendance at the Garden was respectable, the hard-core season ticket-holders remained faithful, but interest in a crowded sports market was waning. The Sox still hadn't won since Ruth was sold to the Yanks, but now the Celtics and Patriots were vying for attention and the public's disposable income. The Bruins had Willie O'Ree, the first black player in the NHL, and the Uke Line of Vic Stasiuk, Bronco Horvath and John Bucyk, but overall the mid-'50s and mid-'60s were glum days.

Then came Bobby Orr.

"I have this saying," said

An iconic moment was frozen in time as Bobby Orr, tripped by St. Louis defenseman Noel Picard, flew through the air after scoring in overtime to win the 1970 Stanley Cup.

Phil Esposito, Fred Stanfield, and Gary Doak (left to right) enjoyed the taste of victory in 1970.

1970

Fans lined the city streets for a raucous parade honoring Bobby Orr, waving, and his teammates after they won the Cup.

Schmidt, who was the Bruins' head coach at the start of the '60s, when the club began scouting Orr as a 12-year-old in Parry Sound, Ontario. "If anybody else comes along that's better than Orr, I hope the Good Lord sees fit to keep me on this earth to watch him — because he will be something else."

It was Orr's arrival in the fall of '66, along with the May 15, 1967, trade with Chicago for Phil Esposito, Ken Hodge, and Fred Stanfield, that brought the Bruins back to days of glory. This time the fervor exceeded even that of the earlier Cup years. With the young Harry Sinden their coach, the swashbuckling and talented Bruins piled up scoring records, with Orr skating and contributing on offense like no defenseman in the history of the game. The Bruins of the late '60s and early '70s were a special team.

Night after night, crazed fans packed the Garden to see Orr and Espo, Derek (Turk) Sanderson and Johnny (Pie) McKenzie, the heroics of Gerry (Cheesie) Cheevers behind his mock-stitched goalie's mask.

"Jesus Saves," read the most popular bumper sticker of the day, "and Espo scores on the rebound." The Garden was a church and the Bruins the deities.

On May 10, 1970, Sanderson and Orr teamed up for the most memorable goal in the franchise's history. Tied with the St. Louis Blues, 3-3, in overtime at Boston Garden, Orr fed a pass to Sanderson in the right corner and cut out of the faceoff circle to collect Sanderson's pass and knock it by goalie Glenn Hall for the Bruins' first Cup since '41. The picture of Orr flying through the air, upended by defenseman Noel Picard, lives on in memories and on barroom walls across New England.

Two years later, the Bruins won the Cup again, this time at Madison Square Garden. But time, the rival World Hockey Association and NHL expansion already were conspiring, all poised to cripple Boston's dreams for more Cups. There have been good days since, including trips to the finals in 1988 and '90. The Bruins got a new arena in 1995. But the days of Orr and the old Garden euphoria have never been repeated.

Until now.

RPHEUM
GRANTS
THE
E.B. HORN
CO.
JEWELERS
YEARS
GILCHRIST
1970

1970 Amid the shower of confetti, fans got close enough to their heroes to reach into the car that also carried the Stanley Cup.

The Bruins let a 5-1 cushion slip away in Game 1 of the finals against the New York Rangers before Ace Bailey came to the rescue, beating Ed Giacomin to score the winning goal in the waning moments.

1972

In Game 3, Wayne Cashman (top) was denied by Giacomin and the Bruins lost, 5-2. But Boston rallied to win the series in Game 6, igniting a memorable party at City Hall.

CLOSE CALLS A FEW WHO FELL JUST SHORT

It was Guy Lafleur and the Montreal Canadiens in 1977 and '78. Edmonton's Mark Messier did the honors in 1990. And if not for a power failure during the 1988 finals, Wayne Gretzky might have paraded the Stanley Cup around Boston Garden ice. Present company excluded, the Bruins reached five finals after 1972, only to come up empty against some of the greatest teams in NHL history.

They were favored to defeat the Philadelphia Flyers in 1974, but not even Bobby Orr and Phil Esposito could prevent a 1-0 shutout at the hands of goalie Bernie Parent in a Cup-clinching Game 6.

A vastly different roster took on mighty Montreal in 1977. The colorful Don Cherry was behind the bench, and the stars were Terry O'Reilly, Brad Park, and Jean Ratelle. But the Canadiens, losers of only eight regular season games, predictably swept the Bruins. A rematch the following spring didn't go much better. Although the Bruins fought back from a 2-0 deficit to deadlock the series, they dropped consecutive 4-1 affairs to fall short once more.

It was déjà vu all over again against the Canadiens in 1979, this time in the Eastern Conference finals. The closing two minutes of regulation in Game 7 at the Montreal Forum are among the most gut-wrenching in franchise history. A Bruins' penalty for too many men on the ice led to Lafleur's game-tying goal, and the Canadiens won in overtime.

With Ray Bourque and Cam Neely leading the way, the Bruins finally ended the Canadiens' curse en route to the 1988 finals, defeating their hated rivals in the playoffs for the first time in 45 years. Still, they were no match for Edmonton, losing in four straight. The most memorable moment was the Boston Garden blackout that forced suspension of Game 4. The series shifted to Edmonton, where the Oilers completed the sweep.

The Oilers derailed Boston's hopes once again two years later. The opening game at the Garden was the longest in finals history, stretching into triple overtime. Edmonton's Petr Klima won the game at 15:13 of the third OT, and the Bruins never recovered, dropping the series in five. It would be 21 long years before the Stanley Cup finals returned to Boston.

In the Great Blackout of 1988 (above left), Boston Garden went dark during Game 4 of the finals against Edmonton, forcing play to be suspended. At right (from top) franchise legends Terry O'Reilly, Ray Bourque, and Cam Neely each played in two finals, but never got their hands on the Stanley Cup as members of the Bruins. Bourque eventually held aloft the silver chalice after being traded to Colorado.

While Bruins' fans ultimately had to wait 39 years between championships, they shared in the jubilation of winning the Stanley Cup when former Bruins' captain Ray Bourque brought the trophy to Boston's City Hall Plaza after his win with Colorado in 2001.

COMPLETE
COMPLETE

THE TROPHY

THINK OF A PUNCH BOWL MOUNTED AT THE EYEPIECE END OF AN ASTRONOMER'S OVERSIZED, CHUNKY TELESCOPE.

KEVIN PAUL DUPONT
Globe Staff

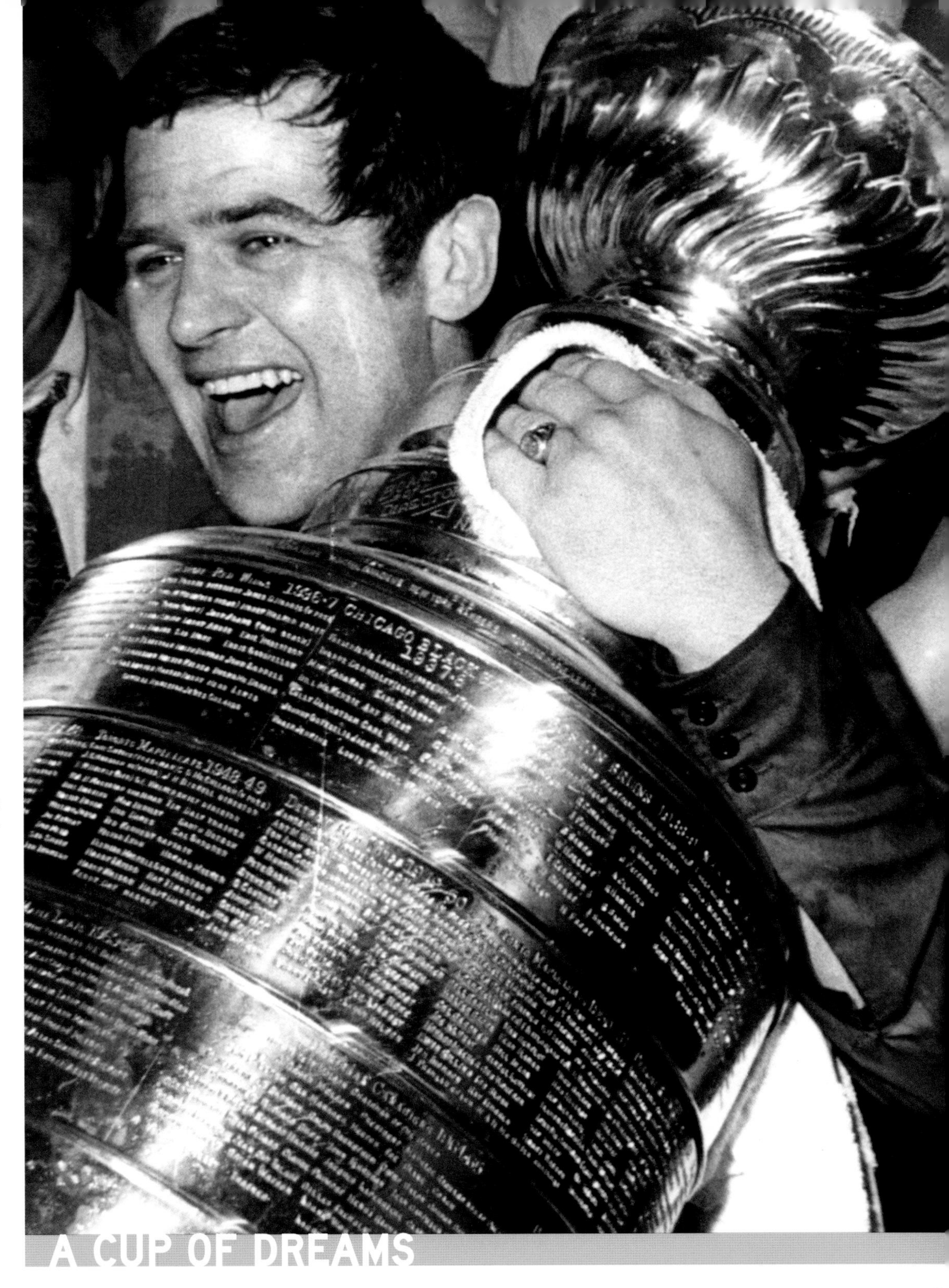

A CUP OF DREAMS

Bearded, worn-out, grizzled men alternately whoop and whimper at its sight.

By far the most recognized trophy in all of North American sports, and among the most identifiable throughout the world, the Stanley Cup inspires greatness, summons tears, and perhaps most of all, represents the crowning achievement of what is arguably the hardest, most grueling championship to win.

Today's version of the Cup weighs 34 1/2 pounds and is 35 1/4 inches high. Think of a punch bowl mounted at the eyepiece end of an astronomer's oversized, chunky telescope. The bowl was a gift from England, presented in 1894 to Canada's best amateur hockey team, the Montreal Amateur Athletic Association. Great Britain's Governor General to Canada, Sir Frederick Arthur Stanley of Preston, was the father of the idea, and purchased the bowl for 10 guineas — a sum of slightly less than $50 at the time — from a silversmith in London.

The original punch bowl, lined in gold, measured 7 1/2 inches high and 11 1/2 inches across, and was retired to a vault in the Hockey Hall of Fame in Toronto in the late 1960s after it became too old and brittle to be lugged safely from hockey barn to hockey barn. It is permanently housed in a glass display case in the HHOF museum, along with a number of the retired bands that bear the engraved names of the Cup's winners through the decades.

When the bottom of the five largest bands that form the Cup's base fills up with names, the top band is removed — retired to the vault — and a blank band added at the bottom for the names of future Cup winners. The other four bands shingle up, closer to the hallowed Cup. The current bottom band, which will have the Bruins' names etched in it this summer by official engraver Louise St. Jacques, began with the 2004-05 season, the only NHL season entirely lost to job action (owners' lockout). It reads, "Season Cancelled."

Once the Cup is clinched, it almost immediately goes on tour, each player of the winning team granted his day with it in the city of his choosing. In 2001 ex-Boston captain/icon Ray Bourque brought his Colorado Cup to Boston City Hall for a crowd of thousands to share his joy. Otherwise, until this year, the Cup hadn't taken a bow in the Hub of Hockey since 1972.

"It's been that one piece missing for a while now. People are waiting for it," Bruins wingman Mark Recchi said during the 2011 playoffs. "... We want to give it to 'em."

It's had its day with (left to right) Phil Esposito, Johnny Bucyk, and Harry Sinden. Now the Stanley Cup has been cuddled and kissed by a whole new generation of Bruins players and coaches.

Bobby Orr (left) and Terry O'Reilly (right) helped Milt Schmidt off the ice after the trio of Bruins legends skated at Fenway Park during festivities at the 2010 Winter Classic.

EMC LEVEL
Winter
CLASSIC
BOSTON-2010

FORWARDS

37 PATRICE BERGERON
Ancienne-Lorette, Quebec, CAN

HT	WT	DOB
6' 2"	194	07-24-1985

11 GREGORY CAMPBELL
London, Ontario, CAN

HT	WT	DOB
6' 0"	197	12-17-1983

18 NATHAN HORTON
Welland, Ontario, CAN

HT	WT	DOB
6' 2"	229	05-29-1985

23 CHRIS KELLY
Toronto, Ontario, CAN

HT	WT	DOB
6' 0"	198	11-11-1980

46 DAVID KREJCI
Sternberk, CZE

HT	WT	DOB
6' 0"	177	04-28-1986

17 MILAN LUCIC
Vancouver, BC, CAN

HT	WT	DOB
6' 4"	220	06-07-1988

63 BRAD MARCHAND
Halifax, Nova Scotia, CAN

HT	WT	DOB
5' 9"	183	05-11-1988

20 DANIEL PAILLE
Welland, Ontario, CAN

HT	WT	DOB
6' 0"	200	04-15-1984

49 RICH PEVERLEY
Kingston, Ontario, CAN

HT	WT	DOB
6' 0"	195	07-08-1982

28 MARK RECCHI
Kamloops, BC, CAN

HT	WT	DOB
5' 10"	195	02-01-1968

73 MICHAEL RYDER
Bonavista, NL, CAN

HT	WT	DOB
6' 0"	186	03-31-1980

91 MARC SAVARD
Ottawa, Ontario, CAN

HT	WT	DOB
5' 10"	191	07-17-1977

19 TYLER SEGUIN
Brampton, Ontario, CAN

HT	WT	DOB
6' 1"	182	01-31-1992

22 SHAWN THORNTON
Oshawa, Ontario, CAN

HT	WT	DOB
6' 2"	217	07-23-1977

DEFENSEMEN

MATT BARTKOWSKI
Pittsburgh, PA, USA

HT	WT	DOB
6' 1"	196	06-04-1988

JOHNNY BOYCHUK
Edmonton, Alberta, CAN

HT	WT	DOB
6' 2"	225	01-19-1984

ZDENO CHARA
Trencin, SVK

HT	WT	DOB
6' 9"	255	03-18-1977

ANDREW FERENCE
Edmonton, Alberta, CAN

HT	WT	DOB
5' 11"	189	03-17-1979

SHANE HNIDY
Neepawa, Manitoba, CAN

HT	WT	DOB
6' 2"	204	11-08-1975

TOMAS KABERLE
Rakovnik, CZE

HT	WT	DOB
6' 1"	214	03-02-1978

STEVEN KAMPFER
Ann Arbor, MI, USA

HT	WT	DOB
5' 11"	197	09-24-1988

ADAM McQUAID
Charlottetown, PE, CAN

HT	WT	DOB
6' 4"	197	10-12-1986

DENNIS SEIDENBERG
Schwenningen, DEU

HT	WT	DOB
6' 1"	210	07-18-1981

GOALIES

ANTON KHUDOBIN
Ust-Kamenogorsk, KAZ

HT	WT	DOB
5' 11"	203	05-07-1986

TUUKKA RASK
Savonlinna, Finland

HT	WT	DOB
6' 3"	169	03-10-1987

TIM THOMAS
Flint, MI, USA

HT	WT	DOB
5' 11"	201	04-15-1974

COACH

CLAUDE JULIEN
Blind River, Ontario, CAN

DOB
04-23-1960

2010/2011 REGULAR SEASON

DATE	OPPONENT		SCORE	PLACE	UP/DOWN	NOTABLE
10-9	Phoenix (@Prague)	L	5-2	4th	**-4**	Local hero Radim Vrbata scored twice to lead Coyotes.
10-10	Phoenix (@Prague	W	3-0	2nd	**-2**	Nathan Horton tallied third goal in two games.
10-16	@New Jersey	W	4-1	3rd	**-4**	Rookie Jordan Caron pocketed first NHL goal.
10-19	@Washington	W	3-1	3rd	**-3**	Tim Thomas made 35 saves as exhausting road trip concluded.
10-21	Washington	W	4-1	2nd	**-1**	Thomas's 38 saves and Horton's fourth goal led in home opener.
10-23	NY Rangers	L	3-2	3rd	**-1**	Marc Staal's breakaway snapped Bruins' four-game winning streak.
10-28	Toronto	W	2-0	3rd	**-3**	Tyler Seguin thrilled Garden crowd with first goal.
10-30	@Ottawa	W	4-0	2nd	**-3**	Thomas improved to 6-0 with second straight shutout.
11-3	@Buffalo	W	5-2	2nd	**-1**	Brad Marchand and Michael Ryder each collected two points.
11-5	@Washington	L	5-3	2nd	**-3**	Bruins erased three-goal deficit before losing.
11-6	St. Louis	O(SO)	1-1	2nd	**-2**	Bruins hit four posts in shootout defeat.
11-10	@Pittsburgh	W	7-4	2nd	**-2**	Five-goal third period stunned Penguins.
11-11	Montreal	L	3-1	2nd	**-4**	Carey Price (34 saves) stoned Bruins.
11-13	Ottawa	L	2-0	3rd	**-6**	Senators handed Thomas first loss.
11-15	New Jersey	W	3-0	2nd	**-4**	Thomas rebounded with fourth shutout.
11-17	@NY Rangers	W	3-2	2nd	**-4**	Bruins improved to 7-1 on the road.
11-18	Florida	W	4-0	2nd	**-2**	Tuukka Rask made 41 saves in first win.
11-20	Los Angeles	O(SO)	3-3	2nd	**-3**	Kings prevailed in sixth round of shootout.
11-22	@Tampa Bay	L	3-1	2nd	**-3**	Steven Stamkos scored league-leading 20th goal.
11-24	@Florida	W	3-1	2nd	**-3**	Mark Recchi reached 1,500 career points.
11-26	Carolina	L	3-0	2nd	**-3**	Hurricanes went three-for-three on the power play.
11-28	@Atlanta	L	4-1	2nd	**-5**	Bruins fell to 0-5-2 when trailing after first period.
12-1	@Philadelphia	W	3-0	2nd	**-4**	Thomas stopped penalty shot, made 41 saves.
12-2	Tampa Bay	W	8-1	2nd	**-4**	Marc Savard returned, David Krejci scored twice in season's biggest rout.
12-4	@Toronto	O(SO)	2-2	2nd	**-5**	Former Bruin Phil Kessel netted winner in shootout.
12-7	Buffalo	W(OT)	3-2	2nd	**-5**	Recchi tipped in Dennis Seidenberg's slapshot in OT.
12-9	NY Islanders	W	5-2	2nd	**-3**	Milan Lucic scored two goals, Rask with 33 saves.
12-11	Philadelphia	O(OT)	2-1	2nd	**-2**	Mike Richards won it for Flyers with three seconds left in OT.
12-15	@Buffalo	L	3-2	2nd	**-2**	Buffalo's Drew Stafford collected hat trick.
12-16	@Montreal	L	4-3	2nd	**-4**	Canadiens kept Bruins in second place.
12-18	Washington	W	3-2	2nd	**-2**	Andrew Ference scored first goal in 100 games.
12-20	Anaheim	L	3-0	2nd	**-2**	Jonas Hiller denied Bruins with 45 saves.
12-23	Atlanta	W	4-1	2nd	**-2**	Shawn Thornton scored twice, game ended with melee.
12-27	@Florida	W(SO)	2-2	1st	**T**	Blake Wheeler's shootout goal put Bruins in first.
12-28	@Tampa Bay	W	4-3	1st	**+2**	Recchi tallied with 19.7 seconds remaining.
12-30	@Atlanta	O(SO)	2-2	1st	**+3**	Winning streak snapped at three.
1-1	@Buffalo	O(SO)	6-6	1st	**+2**	Stafford tied it with 28 seconds left, Sabres won in shootout.
1-3	@Toronto	W	2-1	1st	**+3**	Savard's winner capped 3-0-2 road trip.
1-6	Minnesota	L	3-1	1st	**+1**	Phantom hooking call on Thornton proved costly.
1-8	@Montreal	O(OT)	3-2	1st	**T**	Max Pacioretty's OT goal tied Canadiens for first.
1-10	@Pittsburgh	W	4-2	1st	**+2**	Four goals in final three and a half minutes shocked Penguins.

DATE	OPPONENT		SCORE	PLACE	UP/DOWN	NOTABLE
1-11	Ottawa	W	6-0	1st	**+2**	Patrice Bergeron netted first career hat trick.
1-13	Philadelphia	W	7-5	1st	**+4**	With five-goal third period, Bruins were 7-1-3 in last 11.
1-15	Pittsburgh	L	3-2	1st	**+2**	Seidenberg, Ryder scored 13 seconds apart to erase 2-0 deficit.
1-17	Carolina	W	7-0	1st	**+2**	Zdeno Chara had hat trick, Thomas posted seventh shutout.
1-18	@Carolina	W	3-2	1st	**+3**	A season-high 43 saves for Thomas.
1-20	Buffalo	L	4-2	1st	**+3**	Bruins lost for second time in 23 games when scoring first.
1-22	@Colorado	W	6-2	1st	**+2**	Lucic, Marchand each scored twice.
1-24	@Los Angeles	L	2-0	1st	**+2**	Kings snapped 0-for-22 power play drought.
1-26	Florida	W	2-1	1st	**+4**	Thomas headed to All-Star game with 1.81 goals-against-average.
2-1	@Carolina	W	3-2	1st	**+4**	Bergeron potted the game-winner.
2-3	Dallas	W	6-3	1st	**+4**	Three fights in first four seconds were prelude to victory.
2-5	San Jose	L	2-0	1st	**+2**	Sharks won despite just 18 shots.
2-9	Montreal	W	8-6	1st	**+4**	Even goalies Thomas and Price fought in penalty-filled brawl.
2-11	Detroit	L	6-1	1st	**+3**	Red Wings scored on first two shots.
2-13	@Detroit	L	4-2	1st	**+1**	Second-period shot advantage of 19-6 spurred Red Wings.
2-15	Toronto	L	4-3	1st	**T**	Bruins lost three straight for only time all season.
2-17	@NY Islanders	W	6-3	1st	**+2**	Rask stopped 34, six Bruins scored goals.
2-18	@Ottawa	W	4-2	1st	**+4**	Marchand's two goals highlighted three-goal third period.
2-22	@Calgary	W	3-1	1st	**+4**	Thomas back after week off, lowered goals-against to 1.99.
2-26	@Vancouver	W	3-1	1st	**+4**	Lucic netted winner in lone meeting between Cup finalists.
2-27	@Edmonton	W	3-2	1st	**+6**	Bruins posted 40-17 shot cushion.
3-1	@Ottawa	W	1-0	1st	**+6**	Rask earned shutout, Bruins completed 6-0 road trip.
3-3	Tampa Bay	W	2-1	1st	**+6**	Seventh straight win lifted B's to No. 2 in East.
3-5	Pittsburgh	O(OT)	3-2	1st	**+5**	Streak snapped on Dustin Jeffrey's OT goal.
3-8	@Montreal	L	4-1	1st	**+3**	Game marred by Chara's hit on Pacioretty.
3-10	Buffalo	O(OT)	4-3	1st	**+4**	Brad Boyes beat Bruins in overtime.
3-11	@NY Islanders	L	4-2	1st	**+4**	Islanders scored three in the third.
3-15	@Columbus	W(SO)	2-2	1st	**+4**	Seguin was only player to tally in shootout.
3-17	@Nashville	O(OT)	4-3	1st	**+3**	Shea Weber scored for Maple Leafs with 1:23 left.
3-19	@Toronto	L	5-2	1st	**+3**	Bruins 1-3-3 in last seven games.
3-22	New Jersey	W	4-1	1st	**+3**	Chara collected game-winner to stop slide.
3-24	Montreal	W	7-0	1st	**+5**	Gregory Campbell scored with B's at 5-on-3 disadvantage.
3-26	NY Rangers	L	1-0	1st	**+5**	Rangers goalie Henrik Lundqvist was unbeatable.
3-27	@Philadelphia	W	2-1	1st	**+7**	Marchand won it with 3:43 left.
3-29	Chicago	W	3-0	1st	**+7**	Recchi moved to 12th on all-time scoring list.
3-31	Toronto	O(SO)	3-3	1st	**+8**	Bruins clinched tie for Northeast Division title.
4-2	Atlanta	W	3-2	1st	**+8**	Ryder scored on penalty shot.
4-4	@NY Rangers	L	5-3	1st	**+8**	Rangers erased 3-0 deficit.
4-6	NY Islanders	W	3-2	1st	**+8**	Thornton scored as first period ended.
4-9	Ottawa	W	3-1	1st	**+7**	Thomas set save-percentage record at .938.
4-10	@New Jersey	L	3-2	1st	**+7**	Devils coach Jacques Lemaire retired with a win.

BOSTON BRUINS SEASON HISTORY [1924–2011]

YEAR	PCT.	POINTS	PLACE	RESULT
2010-11	**.628**	**103**	**1st**	**Won Stanley Cup finals**
2009-10	.555	91	3rd	Lost NHL conference quarterfinals
2008-09	.707	116	1st	Lost NHL conference quarterfinals
2007-08	.573	94	3rd	Lost NHL conference quarterfinals
2006-07	.463	76	5th	
2005-06	.451	74	5th	
2004-05 LOCKOUT				
2003-04	.634	104	1st	Lost NHL conference quarterfinals
2002-03	.530	87	3rd	Lost NHL conference quarterfinals
2001-02	.616	101	1st	Lost NHL conference quarterfinals
2000-01	.537	88	4th	
1999-00	.445	73	5th	
1998-99	.555	91	3rd	Lost NHL conference semifinals
1997-98	.555	91	2nd	Lost NHL conference quarterfinals
1996-97	.372	61	6th	
1995-96	.555	91	2nd	Lost NHL conference quarterfinals
1994-95	.594	57	3rd	Lost NHL conference quarterfinals
1993-94	.577	97	2nd	Lost NHL conference semifinals
1992-93	.649	109	1st	Lost NHL division semifinals
1991-92	.525	84	2nd	Lost NHL conference finals
1990-91	.625	100	1st	Lost NHL conference finals
1989-90	.631	101	1st	Lost Stanley Cup finals
1988-89	.550	88	2nd	Lost NHL division finals
1987-88	.588	94	2nd	Lost Stanley Cup finals
1986-87	.531	85	3rd	Lost NHL division semifinals
1985-86	.538	86	3rd	Lost NHL division semifinals
1984-85	.513	82	4th	Lost NHL division semifinals
1983-84	.650	104	1st	Lost NHL division semifinals
1982-83	.688	110	1st	Lost NHL conference finals
1981-82	.600	96	2nd	Lost NHL division finals
1980-81	.544	87	2nd	Lost NHL preliminary round
1979-80	.656	105	2nd	Lost NHL quarterfinals
1978-79	.625	100	1st	Lost NHL semifinals
1977-78	.706	113	1st	Lost Stanley Cup finals
1976-77	.663	106	1st	Lost Stanley Cup finals
1975-76	.706	113	1st	Lost NHL semifinals
1974-75	.588	94	2nd	Lost NHL preliminary round
1973-74	.724	113	1st	Lost Stanley Cup finals
1972-73	.686	107	2nd	Lost NHL quarterfinals
1971-72	**.763**	**119**	**1st**	**Won Stanley Cup finals**
1970-71	.776	121	1st	Lost NHL quarterfinals
1969-70	**.651**	**99**	**2nd**	**Won Stanley Cup finals**
1968-69	.658	100	2nd	Lost NHL semifinals
1967-68	.568	84	3rd	Lost NHL quarterfinals

YEAR	PCT.	POINTS	PLACE	RESULT
1966-67	.314	44	6th	
1965-66	.343	48	5th	
1964-65	.343	48	6th	
1963-64	.343	48	6th	
1962-63	.321	45	6th	
1961-62	.271	38	6th	
1960-61	.307	43	6th	
1959-60	.457	64	5th	
1958-59	.521	73	2nd	Lost NHL semifinals
1957-58	.493	69	4th	Lost Stanley Cup finals
1956-57	.571	80	3rd	Lost Stanley Cup finals
1955-56	.421	59	5th	
1954-55	.479	67	4th	Lost NHL semifinals
1953-54	.529	74	4th	Lost NHL semifinals
1952-53	.493	69	3rd	Lost Stanley Cup finals
1951-52	.471	66	4th	Lost NHL semifinals
1950-51	.443	62	4th	Lost NHL semifinals
1949-50	.429	60	5th	
1948-49	.550	66	2nd	Lost NHL semifinals
1947-48	.492	59	3rd	Lost NHL semifinals
1946-47	.525	63	3rd	Lost NHL semifinals
1945-46	.560	56	2nd	Lost Stanley Cup finals
1944-45	.360	36	4th	Lost NHL semifinals
1943-44	.430	43	5th	
1942-43	.570	57	2nd	Lost Stanley Cup finals
1941-42	.583	56	3rd	Lost NHL semifinals
1940-41	**.698**	**67**	**1st**	**Won Stanley Cup finals**
1939-40	.698	67	1st	Lost NHL semifinals
1938-39	**.771**	**74**	**1st**	**Won Stanley Cup finals**
1937-38	.698	67	1st	Lost NHL semifinals
1936-37	.552	53	2nd	Lost NHL quarterfinals
1935-36	.521	50	2nd	Lost NHL quarterfinals
1934-35	.604	58	1st	Lost NHL semifinals
1933-34	.427	41	4th	
1932-33	.604	58	1st	Lost NHL semifinals
1931-32	.438	42	4th	
1930-31	.705	62	1st	Lost NHL semifinals
1929-30	.875	77	1st	Lost Stanley Cup finals
1928-29	**.648**	**57**	**1st**	**Won Stanley Cup finals**
1927-28	.580	51	1st	Lost NHL semifinals
1926-27	.511	45	2nd	Lost Stanley Cup finals
1925-26	.528	38	4th	
1924-25	.200	12	6th	

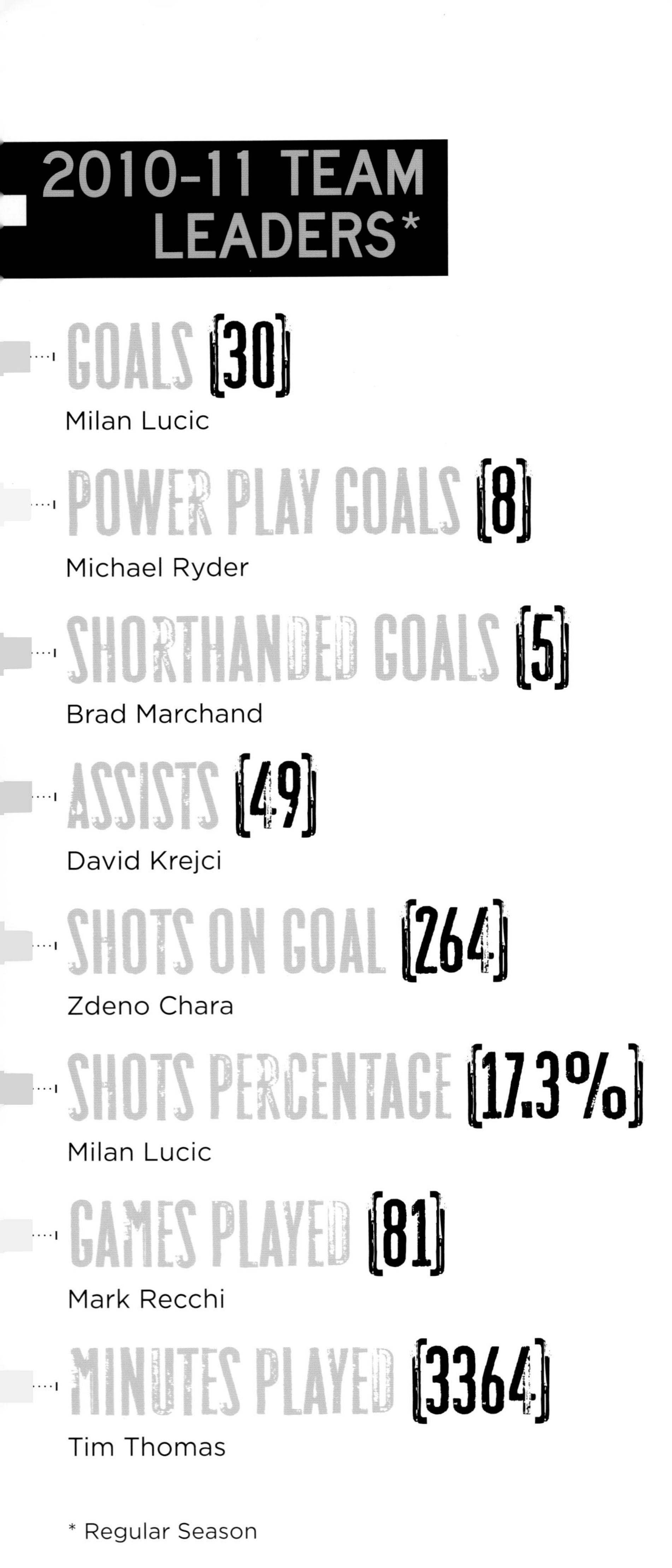

2010-11 TEAM LEADERS*

GOALS [30]
Milan Lucic

POWER PLAY GOALS [8]
Michael Ryder

SHORTHANDED GOALS [5]
Brad Marchand

ASSISTS [49]
David Krejci

SHOTS ON GOAL [264]
Zdeno Chara

SHOTS PERCENTAGE [17.3%]
Milan Lucic

GAMES PLAYED [81]
Mark Recchi

MINUTES PLAYED [3364]
Tim Thomas

* Regular Season

BOSTON BREWIN'
BULLY HILL
Reebok
WARRIOR

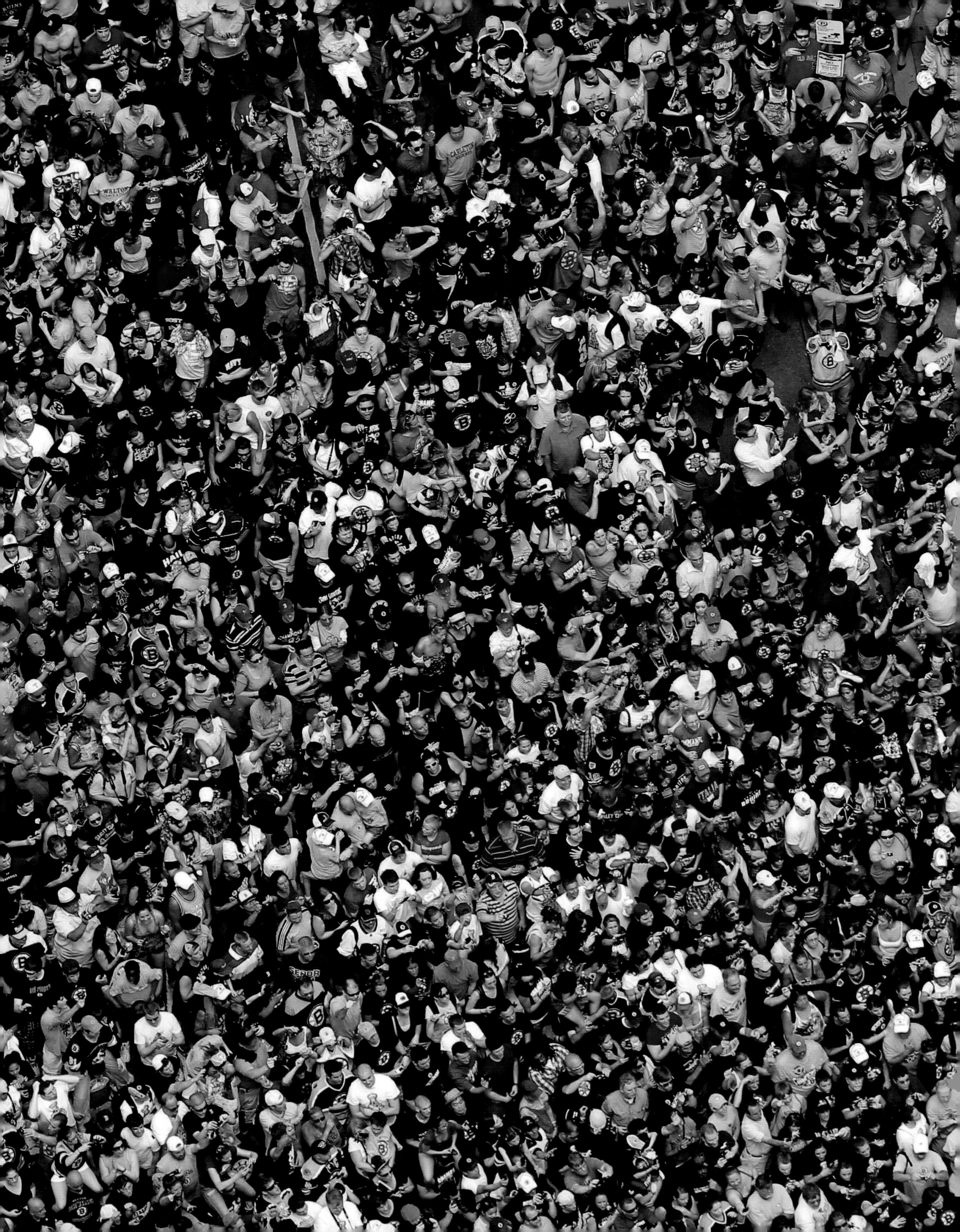

BRUINS
BRUINS

STANLEY CUP
20 11
CHAMPIONS
2011
STANLEY CUP
FINAL

Brad Marchand was in the middle of numerous Bruins' celebrations in the days following their Stanley Cup championship, including this photo with a few of his teammates before the Rolling Rally got underway. Homemade versions of the Stanley Cup were on display all along the parade route.

COPLEY SQUARE

JCDecaux

VIVA

The Bruins' championship banner at the old John Hancock Tower (above) made for an awesome sight, particularly from the vantage point of the flagpole. Meanwhile, Bruins' attire could be found on just about everyone and everything, including statues of (left to right) Paul Revere, "Make Way for Ducklings" characters, and Red Auerbach.

Tim Thomas was the MVP of the playoffs and No. 1 in the hearts of many fans who watched the Rolling Rally from city sidewalks. Others enjoyed the parade from their apartments, which for one day served as the equivalent of luxury boxes in the City of Champions.

BRUINS
BRUINS

BOSTON
33

BRAVO,

BOSTON.